T0292983

THE FREELANCE MINDSET

THE FREELANCE MINDSET

Unleashing Your Side Hustles for Better Work, Play, and Life

JOY BATRA

ROWMAN & LITTLEFIELD
Lanham • Boulder • New York • London

Published by Rowman & Littlefield
An imprint of The Rowman & Littlefield Publishing Group, Inc.
4501 Forbes Boulevard, Suite 200, Lanham, Maryland 20706
www.rowman.com

86-90 Paul Street, London EC2A 4NE

British Library Cataloguing in Publication Information Available

Library of Congress Cataloging-in-Publication Data

Names: Batra, Joy, 1987– author.
Title: The freelance mindset : unleashing your side hustles for better work, play, and life / Joy Batra.
Description: Lanham : Rowman & Littlefield, [2023] | Includes bibliographical references and index.
Identifiers: LCCN 2022028485 (print) | LCCN 2022028486 (ebook) | ISBN 9781538167700 (cloth) | ISBN 9781538167717 (ebook)
Subjects: LCSH: Gig economy. | Part-time employment. | Work-life balance.
Classification: LCC HD5110 .B37 2023 (print) | LCC HD5110 (ebook) | DDC 331.25/727--dc23/eng/20220617
LC record available at https://lccn.loc.gov/2022028485
LC ebook record available at https://lccn.loc.gov/2022028486

For anybody who has ever felt lost because their career didn't look like what they planned.
I'm rooting for you.

For any of [illegible] who [illegible] grown into becoming [illegible]
[illegible] career didn't track like what they planned,
[illegible] is for you.

CONTENTS

Introduction ix

Part I: Crossing the Threshold

1 Why Freelance? *3*

2 What's Risk Got to Do with It? *13*

3 Making the Leap *25*

Part II: Navigating the Trail

4 Uncovering Your Specialty *39*

5 Creating Your Business Plan *53*

6 Dealing with Scarcity and Windfalls *65*

Part III: Becoming a Hero

7 Identity and What Do You Do? *83*

8 Growth and Development *95*

9 What Happens When You Succeed? *111*

Part IV: The Future

10 When Is It Time for a Change? *125*

11 Your Freelance Journey Transforms You *137*

12 The Freelancer's Future *149*

Conclusion 157
Acknowledgments 159
Notes 163
Bibliography 181
Index 195
About the Author 207

INTRODUCTION

I never thought I'd be a freelancer. Growing up, I wanted to be a detective, an artist, and eventually a lawyer. Once I settled on that goal, I didn't question it. I loved the way lawyers talked and thought, the way they used words so carefully. I loved my parents' proud smiles at the idea. As immigrants, security and prestige often seemed just out of reach for them, but a law degree could offer both.

Long before I had heard of the law of attraction or manifestation, I bought a postcard of Harvard Law School and stuck it on the wall of my college dorm room. When I was tired and didn't feel like studying, it gave me a burst of energy to keep pushing.

By spring of senior year I was within striking distance of my goal. I had worked my way up from Cs in my freshman year and now had several straight semesters of perfect grades. My free time was a happy daze of rehearsing with my Bollywood dance team, Masti (literally Hindi for "fun").

Our team had just won a big college-wide competition when my parents called from the hospital. My dad had a terminal disease called ALS (amyotrophic lateral sclerosis) and was in the intensive care unit every couple of months. This time he had gone for a short operation but woke up to the news that he would die within hours without life support.

The semester ended in a blur. I finished my final exams, maintained my 4.0, and graduated. Only now, I wasn't sure I wanted to go to law school. Life suddenly felt short, and I wanted to explore what else was out there. I briefly floated the idea of doing something different—maybe business school?—to my dad, but he was not open to revising my life plan in the limited time he had left. It was too risky. We decided I would take the law school admissions test while he was still alive. Then we would say our goodbyes and he would stop life support.

Everything went according to plan, except when we removed the life support. He lived. What was meant to be two hours stretched to two days, then three, then six. That day, my test results arrived. I unexpectedly scored in the 99th percentile and would have a real shot at getting into our dream school.

"Dad!" I showed him the letter. "I can go to Harvard!"

He smiled and patted my hand.

Two hours later he was dead. Try as I might, I couldn't shake the feeling that he was waiting for those test results to come before he passed on.

The following year I started at Harvard Law School, but I longed to do more than law. I applied to business school and was accepted to Harvard's joint JD/MBA degree program. I thought now my life would finally click, but I felt more lost than ever. I found myself scrolling social media in the library when I should have been studying instead. The captain of my college dance team had become a Bollywood actress, and her posts showed her dancing under palm trees. I wanted to feel as carefree as she looked.

But I didn't dare tell anyone. Who would understand?

When I snagged what seemed like my dream job so many years ago—a position at a fancy law firm—I tried to ignore the gnawing feeling that I wanted a different life. A life filled with adventure.

After graduation I discovered my dance captain's acting school had a course that fit exactly within my break between the bar exam and my new job. Perfect, I thought. I would go, have a quick adventure, and then settle into adult life. I flew to Mumbai and took the class. But I ended up meeting a producer who gave me an audition and, eventually, a talent management contract. Just days before my new job was supposed to start, I had to make a decision: Should I take the traditional job with a secure path or follow an unknown and dangerous road?

My mom was understandably terrified. After all, despite my six-figure loans, we were on the brink of the financial stability she had sacrificed her whole life for. But to me, the acting contract was an escape hatch. It promised the excitement I craved. I declined the job offer and moved to India, bringing my debt with me.

Spoiler alert: I did not become a Bollywood star. This isn't a fairy tale. I acted in some commercials, danced in a film, and got short-listed for some bigger roles that didn't work out. Finding myself with a lot of time and very little cash between auditions, I pitched for part-time consulting projects. After a lot of trial and error, I eventually got hired.

Surprisingly, *this* was the dream. I was finally in the sweet spot I had craved for so long but didn't know existed. I discovered I didn't need to work in a nine-to-five office job to support myself. I could have time to chase my unlikely passions and also pay my bills. I now spent my mornings making Excel spreadsheets and PowerPoint presentations. I loved tackling these complicated corporate problems in smaller doses. Doing the work I had trained my whole life for was grounding. It gave my days structure. In the afternoons I put on heavy makeup and a *salwar kameez* and rode a rickshaw to my auditions. Using a different part of my mind filled me with fresh energy. In the evenings I dined with my extended family before exploring the city with new friends from my acting class. If I had taken any of the jobs I had considered during school, I would not have had so much free time to spend with the people who mattered to me. I would have missed out on getting to know my grandparents before they passed, or being with my friend at the exact moment she discovered she was pregnant.

The story I had heard my whole life—that you go to school then grow up, get a job, and give up all the other parts of yourself—turned out to be fiction. I thought my only options were full-time job or no job. I didn't realize there was a third path in between the two. I delighted in the hidden way of life that was now being revealed to me. This new reality was far more interesting than any fairy tale could be.

Freelancing offered a solution that allowed me to have the best of both worlds. And even though I didn't know any of them at the time, millions of other workers around the world were forging similar pathways into a freelance life on their own terms.

HOW AND WHY I WROTE THIS BOOK

When I first started freelancing, I didn't know anyone else who was doing it. I had to discover this career path for myself, which meant I began freelancing later and with more confusion. And without a role model to guide me, I learned by making a lot of mistakes. At times I felt ashamed, like there was something wrong with me because the idea of a traditional career didn't excite me the way it seemed to do for my classmates.

I recognize that I've been very fortunate in both my educational opportunities, and that there it is a tremendous privilege to be able to turn down a hefty paycheck in order to look for self-actualization. Many gig workers, freelancers, and people with multiple jobs are not doing it by choice. They would love the opportunity to have a full-time job that offers even some of the benefits that others take for granted.

The questions of whether to freelance, how to do it, and when are incredibly personal. Your answers will be driven by your unique circumstances and values. But if you want to explore what a freelance life could look like for you, this book is meant to help.

While researching this book, I interviewed fifty freelancers, founders, and futurists about their experiences with freelancing. They told me why freelancing mattered to them, the biggest surprises of an independent career, as well as their hopes, dreams, and fears about freelancing. Many of them told me they delayed freelancing because they didn't see any examples of other people doing it. I don't want this to be the case for you.

These interviewees held many job titles, including construction workers, baristas, store clerks, teachers, designers, filmmakers, writers, dancers, actors, musicians, engineers, lawyers, doctors, and even a clown. Some considered themselves freelancers. Others felt they were self-employed, solopreneurs, or entrepreneurs. One group saw their careers as portfolios with many components. Another group viewed themselves as having a side hustle or hobby on top of their day jobs.

All these people are freelancers. The self-employed delivery person is as much a freelancer as the thought leader who gives keynote speeches and sits on a board of directors. This is because they are both at the center of their own businesses. They don't work for a company that will look out for their interests in order to retain them. Instead, they are paid to look out for one or more company's interests but must also take care of their own.

There's a lot of tactical information available now about how to start freelancing, create your website, and get your first client. All that information is like a Freelancing 101 course. There's less information about what actually happens once you become a freelancer. That's where this book fits. Think of it as Freelancing 201. It aims to answer the question of what comes next after we begin freelancing. How can we use freelancing to make a living and also build a life we find fulfilling? A life where you can grow in the directions you care about and make space for your many interests and priorities. I call this way of thinking the freelance mindset.

HOW THIS BOOK WILL BENEFIT YOU

This book is for you if you feel lost or stuck in your career, unsatisfied with the day jobs available to you, or if you feel that there are parts of your personality you long to express but don't know how. If you think you are alone in feeling this way, like the outside world does not understand, this book will help you find your tribe. And if you want to take a risk but don't feel equipped to navigate it, this book will help you chart your path.

You are not alone. You *do* have permission to make the changes you crave. You can take a step toward a more satisfying and meaningful life, even if it's something you've never seen anyone else do before.

A FREELANCER'S TRAIL GUIDE

Luckily, on this journey we have some guides. If you have ever watched *Wonder Woman*, *Star Wars*, or *Moana*, you've encountered what is called the hero's journey. This timeless story structure was popularized in the West by Joseph Campbell's 1949 book, *The Hero with a Thousand Faces*, and then iterated and adapted by countless scholars, including Maureen Murdock and Victoria Lynn Schmidt, who developed versions of the heroine's journey.[1]

You, dear reader, are embarking on a heroic journey of your own. If you are questioning your limited view of a career as simply a nine-to-five traditional job, if you are interested in using a freelance mindset to reconnect with your passions, or if you are looking for more freedom and flexibility in your working life, then you have already left the old-world way of thinking.

This book has four parts to match the stages of your journey, from stumbling into a new world to adapting to it, developing a new identity, and then learning to navigate both the new and the old worlds. The stages are presented chronologically, but remember, you are the main character of this journey and can navigate it in any way you like. Feel free to skip to the parts that speak to you and check out the rest another time.

In part 1, "Crossing the Threshold," we find our illusions about the way we work are just that—stories we made up or, worse, stories that were made up for us. The current way of work is, in fact, not working for us. We discover there is another way and, much as we try to resist, we choose the road of adventure, which brings us to a new and disorienting world.

Part 2, "Navigating the Trail," has us do just that. Here we get our bearings. We face trials and feel others' judgmental eyes bear down on us. But we also find support and start discovering what works for us.

The third part, "Becoming a Hero," examines a turning point. We now have the tools we need to exist as either freelancers or traditional employees, but we cannot go back to seeing the world in the limited nine-to-five way we once did. Now we choose again whether to stay on this uncharted path of freelancing, return to traditional employment, or create something new entirely, taking from each world the elements that serve us best.

In part 4, "The Future," we compare traditional employment with the freelance lifestyle and observe the gaps between the two. We explore new models for incorporating the freelance mindset into our professional and personal lives in order to create a more sustainable future.

Are you ready to unlock a whole new way of thinking about your work, play, and life? If so, let's begin.

I

CROSSING THE THRESHOLD

1

WHY FREELANCE?

The circus was once a majestic big-top affair where dozens of daring performers crowded onto a three-ring stage. This was how David Dimitri imagined it as a child growing up in the foothills of the Swiss Alps. His father was a famous clown who performed with Marcel Marceau.[1] When David was old enough to join his father on tour, he fell in love with the circus. David knew it was his life's calling. He trained at the State Academy for Circus Arts in Budapest and eventually earned a coveted spot at Juilliard.[2]

David started his postgraduate career as a freelance wire walker, performing in commercials for large brands before securing a steady job at the Metropolitan Opera. There he walked a high wire in the opera *Manon* before moving on to do the same at the Big Apple Circus and eventually Cirque du Soleil.

After more than a decade of performing in large shows, David grew disenchanted with the bureaucracy involved in a large circus operation. A rigid hierarchy separated the director, artists, and crew.[3] The work also started to feel repetitive. "You do a couple flips on the wire and then what?" He said, "I wanted to do more."[4]

David made a decision. He would create his own circus. And so L'homme Cirque (The One-Man Circus) was born.

L'homme Cirque is the first show of its kind. It has only one performer, David, who does all the acts of a traditional circus: high wire, clown, mime, musician, ringmaster.[5] He even shoots himself out of a cannon he spent two years building by hand.[6] Between performances, David also functions as the circus director and technician. He markets his shows himself, sets up and takes down the stage, and even drives the truck for his tours.[7] L'homme Cirque was tremendously successful, touring almost continuously from its creation in 2007 until the coronavirus pandemic began in 2020.[8]

It's thrilling, both for David and the audience, but uniquely challenging. At a large circus there are many performers, so if one gets sick, the show still goes on. But with his own show, the risk falls entirely on him. "You suddenly are your own boss," David said. "It's a big risk and responsibility that you have to take on, and nobody can take it for you."

The work is difficult. It involves traveling alone, being far from home, and setting up and taking down the stage in the rain, snow, and mud. "It's rough," he said. "It can be very rough, the circus." And yet, David would not have it any other way. "The best part is the freedom that you have," he said. "Every night, it was *my* thing that I was doing. It never got boring. It was always a challenge."[9]

David has experienced his own call to adventure, just as hundreds of millions of people around the world have accepted a similar call. Fed up with the bureaucracy and limitations of full-time traditional employment, workers decide to go it alone. When they dip into the waters of freelance work, many people don't realize doing so also means creating and running a business. And many navigate these challenges without a strong support system or community.

FREELANCERS SHARE WHY THEY ACCEPTED THE CALL

Starting his own circus has not been easy for David, but the rewards have been worth it. Even if you are not creating a circus, freelancing can be a challenging road to navigate. As freelance film director Alex Smith said, "Whatever reasons you have for doing it in the first place need to be pretty strong, because they will be tested. Plenty of times."[10] We'll talk more about the specific ways these reasons can be tested later on, but let's start with why we are even drawn to freelancing in the first place.

Financial Freedom

Josue Tovar has been working since he was fourteen, first at McDonald's then at a variety of other businesses. While these jobs offered much-needed income, Josue's prospects for financial growth seemed limited. He had immigrated to the United States from what he describes as "a very poor family in a very poor village in Mexico."[11] For him, freelancing was a path to financial opportunity.

"I was getting tired of using my skills to make someone else money," he told me. "I thought that if I could just work for myself, it would be a lot better. I could grow and make my own company grow."

Josue, now twenty-six years old, is a freelance roofer and the co-founder of a construction company with his three brothers. He is not alone in using freelancing to expand his earning potential. Research shows that freelancers frequently earn more per hour, while also experiencing more flexibility and reporting higher well-being and mental health, than their non-freelancing peers.[12]

For others, freelancing can be more of a stopgap measure. It might help you bolster your finances, tackle high expenses, or plan for the future. One freelance strategy consultant described using side projects to help ease the pressure from student loans. After finishing school, Sam had $100,000 of student loans.[13] An interest rate of 8 percent a year created more than $600 of additional debt every month. By working at a full-time job and also taking on freelance side projects during nights and weekends, Sam was able to reduce the loans and their accompanying stress to a level that felt more manageable. After achieving this goal, Sam eased back on the freelancing but would consider starting it again if needed to save for another, future expense.

While we all have different financial goals and circumstances, for many people—about half of all freelancers—the additional money is our main reason for freelancing. But humans are complex, and money is not the only thing that excites us. Let's discuss two other possible reasons for freelancing.

Creative Fulfillment

You are naturally curious and passionate. As a child, before you needed to think deeply about money, you probably played games, had imaginary friends, and competed in sports. Those instincts might get buried as we grow up, but they don't disappear altogether. Freelancing can be a way to get back in touch with this pure form of ourselves, to stay in touch with our needs to play, grow, and learn.

Ernie Valverde is a creative video editor at an agency and loves it. But as he progressed in his career, his work became more specialized. This meant that parts of the job that once felt novel now seemed almost repetitive. So he turned to freelancing on nights and weekends to go beyond video editing and work on related aspects like video production and motion graphics for clients in different industries. For Ernie, freelancing is a way to practice skills that are related to his day job but are no longer his primary responsibility.

"You need an outlet," he said, "especially when you work in this type of creative field. It's too monotonous to do the same type of work [every day] even if you're being creative within it."[14]

I was surprised to learn that his company actually encourages its employees to take on side projects as long as their day job doesn't suffer. Supporting their employees' outside interests helps keep their workers happy and engaged. And it helps them develop new skills that make them better at their day jobs. As I spoke to more people, I discovered that many companies tend to be more open to their employees' outside work, especially in creative fields, where freelancing is more common.

Author Rose Lake interviewed for and got a full-time job at a magazine while she was writing her first book. Some of her colleagues were also writing books in addition to their jobs, which made them more understanding when Rose used vacation days to go on her first book tour. Several journalists told me they were allowed to write pieces as freelancers for other websites as long as that didn't interfere with their full-time writing jobs. In tech, many worked on side projects outside of their day jobs to get up to speed with new technologies and use cases. For this group, side projects helped them build skills and grow their networks in ways that made them better and more satisfied at their primary work.

For others, freelancing is a way to scratch a creative itch that is completely unrelated to their day jobs. Chelsea Lorraine is a mechanical engineer and also a singer. A talented math and science student since high school, she weighs the balance between security and creativity.

"I chose engineering because of its stability. But I've always wanted to do music," she said.[15]

Her combination of jobs may seem uncommon, but her manager, an engineer who is married to a singer, can understand Chelsea's love for the art form.

"He gets it," she said. "I can have a terrible day. Then I go and teach two voice lessons and feel like a new person. That makes it worth it."

Freelancing offers a breath of fresh air to these workers by allowing them to explore different aspects of their identities and to feel like they are constantly learning and growing.

Autonomy

Working for yourself as a freelancer gives you a different level of autonomy than would be possible in a traditional job. Freelancing can give you ownership over your work, your time, or your career. Let's explore what each of these looks like.

Alex, a freelance film director, decided to work full-time as a freelancer in order to focus his energy on the projects that mattered most to him.

"My real goal is to do movies and TV," he told me. But after graduating from film school, the work available to him was directing videos for social media. He did that at first, but it wasn't what he wanted to do long term.

"There's your goal, and then there's all the suburbs around that goal," he told me. "It's really easy to find yourself halfway, doing something similar but not the exact thing you crave. For fulfillment, that's a pretty dangerous place to be."

After a decade of building up work experience, relationships, and some savings, he decided to go full-time freelance in order to focus on the projects that excited him most.

"It can be fun or daunting," he said. "Personally, I find it fun, like a big adventure."

Beyond the actual work, many freelancers love freelancing for the flexibility it gives you over your own time. Countless interviewees told me how much they appreciated the ability to *decide* when to take a long lunch with friends, travel, run errands, or spend time with family without asking anyone else's permission. This resonated with me. The best part of freelancing for me was being able to make my own schedule and choose whether I wanted to spend my afternoon working from a coffee shop, auditioning, or just going to the beach.

A final group of freelancers were drawn to this lifestyle because it gave them agency over their careers. John Kador, a writer who has been a full-time freelancer for several decades, said, "I started freelancing the way most people of my generation did: I got fired."[16] His wife loves to joke that he is "unemployable" because of his strong independent streak. Freelancing harnesses that independent streak and turns it into a long-term advantage. John thrives by running his own business, setting his goals, and knowing that he is in charge of his destiny.

Why do you want to freelance? Is it to have more money? More variety in your work? More ownership over your career? Maybe a combination of the three? You may want to jot down all the things you hope freelancing can add to your life and your career. They will be your guides as you explore the different kinds and configurations of freelancing to find the one that feels right for you.

A NEW SPIN ON A TIMELESS TRADITION

When freelancing can offer so many benefits to our lives, why do so many of us delay pursuing it? Divya Chhabra, a psychiatrist and writer, spent years not freelancing simply because she didn't know it was an option available to her. She loved helping families as a doctor but longed to also do work that filled her creatively, like writing. She didn't know anyone else working in medicine and the arts at the same time, so for years she thought she needed to pursue just one career or the other.

"I didn't see examples of people who looked like me doing this combination of work. So I never thought that was for me," she said. "And then when I moved to New York, I realized . . . these things are possible."[17]

I similarly felt that my career needed to be binary, just law or just something else. When freelancing appeared as a third path, it was a brand-new revelation. But it turns out that charting your own career, perhaps in a multidisciplinary way, has been around for a long time.

Freelancers first appeared in literature hundreds of years ago. In *Ivanhoe*, a classic novel about the Middle Ages, a feudal lord describes his army of independent soldiers:

"I offered Richard the service of my Free Lances, and he refused them—I will lead them to Hull, seize on shipping, and embark for Flanders; thanks to the bustling times, a man of action will always find employment."[18]

This army of Free Lance soldiers was not beholden to any one employer. Instead, they offered their services to the highest bidder, and refreshed their offerings according to the needs of the day in order to stay ahead of the pack. Although the novel came out in 1820, the phenomenon of freelance soldiers dates at least as far back as CE 1000.[19]

Today's freelancers offer a variety of skills and services. We are often referred to as "slashies" or "multihyphenates," so called for the slashes or hyphens needed for our many titles and careers.[20] While the words are new, today's multihyphenates are just the latest in a long tradition of people with wide interests and varied expertise, with a legacy that dates back thousands of years.

The term "polymath," from the Greek *polumathēs*, "having learned much," harkens back to ancient Greece, a hotbed of polymaths-turned-household-names. Perhaps the most renowned was Aristotle, who weighed in on at least fifteen subject areas, including physics, zoology, ethics, poetry, theater, aesthetics, economics, linguistics, and politics, in the fourth century BCE.[21] And circa 2650 BCE, a full twenty-three hundred years before Aristotle, one of the first polymaths of record was active in ancient Egypt. Imhotep was a chancellor, an architect, and a priest. After death, his legend continued to grow, and eventually he was considered the god of medicine.[22]

Farther east was Zhang Heng, the Chinese polymath who was a noted expert in nearly a dozen diverse fields. If he were a modern-day slashie, his name tag would include *astronomer*, *mathematician*, *inventor*, *geographer*, *artist*, *poet*, and *politician*.[23] One of the earliest female polymaths was Hypatia. Active in the fourth century, she became one of the world's most prominent mathematicians, astronomers, and philosophers.[24]

If you've ever felt alone because you don't know others who had a career like the one you dream of, know that you are not. People have felt the way you do for thousands of years. Today technology makes it easier than ever before to find work across industries and geographies, to meet people in different professions, and discover examples of the work we crave.

Next up in this long tradition is you!

HOW THE FREELANCE MINDSET CAN HELP

Neither freelancing nor traditional employment in its current form can offer a miracle cure to the challenges that capitalism imposes on our daily lives. However, incorporating a freelance mindset can shatter this false dichotomy and crack open a new way of looking at the world and our lives. Rather than simply two options, we have at least four types of employment available to choose from:

- Full-time job
- Full-time job with part-time freelance
- Part-time job with part-time freelance
- Full-time freelance

We can adopt the new belief that no single job will meet all our financial, social, emotional, spiritual, and physical needs. When we acknowledge this reality, we gain agency. The problem isn't that we haven't made it or haven't found our calling or don't hustle enough. Rather, we are living in a system that was never designed with our personal well-being in mind. By acknowledging that, we now have the opportunity to rethink what is important to us. We can decide what we will and will not pursue, and consciously enforce those boundaries.

With a freelance mindset, you integrate your need to pay the bills with your passions, side hustles, and relationships. In other words, instead of focusing only on climbing a corporate ladder, you strive to live a well-rounded life. This mindset is for you if you want to take joy in your outside interests, even though they might not earn as much as your other skills do. If you want to have a say in what, when, and how you work. If you want to invest in yourself and your ability to grow and develop new interests. And if you want to make yourself less dependent on one source of income so that if something goes wrong, there is a backup plan.

Before proceeding, let's get clear about what a freelance mindset actually is. Table 1 outlines both some typical misconceptions about this mindset and some more accurate descriptions.

Table 1.1. What a Freelance Mindset Really Is

A Freelance Mindset Is . . .	For anyone with a side hustle or side interest they hold dear For people who are in the workforce A series of small shifts you can make that add up to something powerful Working in a way that makes time for things that matter for you A mix of delaying gratification and doing that outlandish thing you've always wanted to do
A Freelance Mindset Is Not . . .	Only for people who quit their jobs Restricted to a certain type of person (influencer, super networker, someone with fancy degrees, younger people, older people, wealthier people, . . .) A dramatic lifestyle change Working yourself to the bone while neglecting your personal life Watching your bucket list grow longer and longer while never crossing anything off

With a freelance mindset, you will be able to buffer yourself against the unexpected and elevate the parts of your life you hold dear. This mindset can give you the tools to:

- Tap into your latent creativity;
- Develop multiple sources of income so you are less dependent on any one employer;
- Grow your skills and your network to generate recurring business;
- Cultivate your passion projects and noncorporate interests;
- Integrate your different interests into a single identity;
- Write your own journey, no matter how different it is from what you expected.

This book is your road map. It is your guide. Use it along with your own developing skills and passions to become the best freelancer you can be.

SUMMARY

- Freelancing is taking off because of our strong desire for freedom and autonomy, which traditional employment can rarely satisfy.
- A freelance mindset helps us elevate the aspects of our personal and professional lives we hold dear by allowing us to set our own goals and boundaries instead of having them set for us by an outside party.
- Even though freelancing is an uncertain road, you *do* have permission to add it to your career path.

2

WHAT'S RISK GOT TO DO WITH IT?

The movie *Tick, Tick . . . Boom!* tells the story of the young playwright Jonathan Larson.[1] Long before he wrote the Broadway musical *Rent*, which won a Tony Award and a Pulitzer Prize, he had to answer one critical question: Should he follow his instinct to be a creative, or should he take a corporate job? The question plagues him throughout *Tick, Tick . . . Boom!* as Jonathan struggles to pay rent, eventually losing electricity while working frantic shifts at the Moondance Diner and writing his first play. Michael, his best friend and roommate, takes the opposite approach. Despite being a talented actor, Michael accepts a job in advertising. This job lets him move out of the dilapidated place he shared with Jonathan and into a massive, sun-drenched luxury apartment of his own. In one of the opening scenes, Jonathan is on the brink of giving up, when Michael asks him an important question: "Are you letting yourself be led by fear or by love?"[2]

At the beginning of each great journey, the voyager must decide whether to accept the adventure that is offered. There are a million reasons to say no: The road is dangerous. The task is almost impossible. Going on this adventure would mean leaving behind everything that you have ever known as safe and familiar. And yet . . . it calls to you.

The same thing happens with the journey into freelancing. Until you begin, freelancing feels like an unknown world. Yes, you know what it is—but how will it turn out for *you*? The path is uncertain and marked with pitfalls. You, like Jonathan Larson, have to decide whether to move forward at all. And, if you do, you must decide whether you will be driven by fear or love. We've already explored the love that pulls freelancers toward their careers in the previous chapter, but now let's bring our fears about freelancing into the light so we can see if they are truly as scary as they seem.

WHY WE FEAR FREELANCING

To non-freelancers, the thought of full-time freelancing can sound as frightening as skydiving without a parachute. While we know full-time freelancing is just one of many options, the freelance lifestyle does involve risk. These risks range from financial to physical, and can even be emotional. But is mortal fear warranted? Let's examine the evidence.

Financial Risks

The financial risk of relying on freelancing without a full-time job is top of mind for many people. When you are fully self-employed, as freelancer Vyjayanthi Vadrevu told me, "the risk of starving is real"—especially when you are first starting out.[3]

Vyjayanthi is a freelance actor and anthropologist. Having acted and modeled as a child, art is one way for Vyjayanthi to understand the human condition. Anthropology is another, which she teaches at a university. As an anthropologist, she now helps companies better understand their customers.

The first time Vyjayanthi freelanced full-time in order to pursue acting, she ended up at the last dollar in her bank account. At the time, she had not fully considered the financial aspect because her creative calling was so strong.

"When you have your livelihood or somebody else's at stake, the voice inside of you that's driving you to chase your calling has to be that much stronger," she told me.[4]

She admitted that she had rushed into freelancing without lining up steady work and hadn't saved as diligently as she does now, but that was one of the most difficult points in her career.

"Let's call it what it was: It was hard. I should not have done that," she said.

Her takeaway: Don't just dive into freelancing without a solid financial backup plan, unless you can afford to take that risk. And if you don't have that luxury, try looking for part-time work that can give you consistent income while you grow your base of freelance clients.

Health Concerns

The physical health risks of freelancing apply primarily to the United States, where the social safety net is minimal. Difficulties getting good health insurance can make you question your career choice. I spoke with Jason Jhung, a former freelancer and recreational baseball player, who said that he couldn't afford health insurance early on in his career because it would have cost $1,000 a month.[5] He weighed the expense of insurance against the risk of a torn MCL (a torn medial collateral ligament, a severe knee injury common to baseball players) and needing surgery that would cost at least $7,000—if not several multiples more.[6] An expense that large could lead to cost-cutting elsewhere; for example, forcing a person to forgo physical therapy, checkups, and maybe even food, all while trying to heal from an injury. As many freelancers lack sick pay and disability insurance, a serious illness or physical incapacity from an accident could mean months or years of no income. The decision to freelance should include considerations of how you will care for your physical and mental health in an ongoing way.

Emotional Pitfalls

Many freelancers I spoke with had not predicted how isolated they would feel as freelancers. They missed the office camaraderie and feeling of being on a team much more than they expected. I know I did, especially when doing all my work remotely.

Beyond that baseline of being self-employed, there is also the risk of internalizing feelings of shame and failure if you experience any of the previously described financial and physical worst-case scenarios. These negative feelings can trap you in a painful cycle: You feel as if there is something wrong with you when you're not bringing in enough sales. And then that feeling makes it harder for you to pitch your work confidently, making clients less likely to hire you.

If you start to get down on yourself for things not looking the way you expected, psychiatrist and author Saumya Dave suggests reframing your perspective to acknowledge how your challenges today fit within a wider system that was not created with freelancers in mind.

"Because freelancers are taking these risks, we are able to have the world we have," she said. "Freelancers are making the world better for us, but the world is not set up for them to have an easy time. It is not their fault that is so hard to financially sustain themselves while doing so."[7]

So, there are serious risks. Freelancing by itself is as dangerous as any other heroic journey. You could go broke from insufficient work, suffer because of inadequate or nonexistent health care, or become isolated and unhappy.

But wait. What's the alternative?

THE RISKS OF TRADITIONAL EMPLOYMENT

The other extreme is to become an employee at one full-time job. Some of the risks get better. You will probably have a steady paycheck, insurance, and a team. But is traditional employment really less risky overall? The freelance mindset acknowledges that being a full-time employee is almost as risky as being a full-time freelancer for three reasons. Let's explore them now.

Your Job Is Not Guaranteed

Ask any of the twenty million Americans who lost work during the last recession.[8] Many of them *had* a job. They had supposedly done everything right, played by the rules of the old playbook. And then what happened? They found themselves in that same position of a freelance famine: locked into high expenses and trying to sell their services to company after company while watching the market and their bank balance dwindle. These widespread layoffs and furloughs left millions scrambling for work, which left both workers and businesses more open to freelance projects.[9]

Tamala Baldwin, a freelance writer and producer, told me about her experience with a recession early in her career. She had moved from New York to California for a job. Tamala was settling into her new life and had even found an apartment near the beach that she loved, when she was unexpectedly laid off. The company needed to cut costs.

"I felt like I had no control," Tamala told me. "That's part of the illusion. You think you're in control if you have a full-time job. But I feel more empowered and more in control of my destiny now as a freelancer."[10]

The lesson from these mass layoffs is that you can't rely on a company to take care of you. People who survive downturns have a freelance mindset. Even if they have a full-time job, they already have other clients and are actively pitching to new ones. Freelancing, then, becomes the safety net—not the risk.

Your Upside Is Capped

With the steady paycheck of a traditional job, your losses are more limited. Unfortunately, so are your gains. Some people very strategically, luckily—or both—become fabulously wealthy from their jobs. Most of those people did so by taking on some amount of risk, like founding a company, joining an early-stage start-up, making large investments, or selling on commission.

For the majority, though, the reverse is true. We will be paid some fixed amount—maybe by the hour, maybe by the year. If you're eligible for a bonus or equity, you can usually calculate approximately how much it will be worth. But these amounts are also carefully calculated by your employer, so they usually land in a range that will keep you hungry for more. If the salary is too low, you'll look for a better job. But if it's too high, you could retire.

What kinds of incentives do these employment situations create for employees who know (1) that their job is not guaranteed and (2) roughly what their compensation ceiling is? If you are on a fixed wage, you work a little, you get paid one amount. If you work a lot, you get paid that same amount. Increasing your effort might not always bring you closer to your financial and professional goals, especially if your company has a rigid hierarchy or strict criteria for raises and promotions.

In these situations, looking for additional opportunities beyond your day job can give you the growth you crave. With freelancing, there is no externally imposed limit on what you can achieve. You don't know what you'll be able to sell or how your new skills will be valued by the market. You might dabble in a niche interest like creating videos, only to amass thousands of engaged followers who bring you a steady stream of new business opportunities. They may even make you more valuable to full-time employers. This freelance-forward approach can help you increase your income, develop valuable skills, and even take on leadership roles that might be out of reach in your current organization.

Taking an unknown road is not easy, but it can be tremendously worthwhile.

You Are Missing Out on Experience

If you are one of the very lucky few for whom the previous two risks do not apply, I urge you to ask yourself if you are living your life to the fullest. Yes, we must think about financial matters, but when it comes down to it, money is not what motivates us at our core. We all want to use that money for *something.*

What do you want to explore? Are there other possible lives and versions of yourself that you would like to meet? A freelance mindset lets you do exactly that. Want to tango in Argentina? Build cool apps? Cook a perfect béchamel sauce? Perform *King Lear* on stage? With a freelance mindset, you can explore these possibilities and more. It can't guarantee you will get paid for any of these things, but it will allow you to arrange your finances so that you can have enough time to give them a try. Having the time to spend on our deeply held dreams is a different kind of wealth altogether. That way, when you're on your deathbed, you can be satisfied knowing you really had a full go of this life.

HOW FREELANCING CAN REDUCE SOME RISKS

Refusing to specialize can also improve your job security as a freelancer. Let's explore this with a hypothetical situation. Imagine you are at a woodland resort that has only two vendors. One vendor sells ice cream; the other, hot chocolate. Half of the days in this forest, the weather is warm; the other half, it's cold. As you may imagine, warm days are great for the ice-cream seller. But when the temperature dips, people get in line to buy hot chocolate instead. Of course a few brave souls buy both treats or neither, regardless of temperature, but let's ignore them for simplicity's sake and assume people just buy one or the other.

If you could only work for one of the businesses, which one would you choose? If you chose the ice-cream vendor, you'd be in great luck if all the days are hot. You'd be in trouble, though, if the days turn out to be cold. The reverse would be true if you chose the hot chocolate vendor.

But what if you could work for both companies at the same time? You'd reduce your overall risk and still come out ahead. That way you'd have plenty of work no matter the weather.

This was the idea behind *modern portfolio theory*, which won economist Harry Markowitz the Nobel Prize. This theory is a key reason that *diversify* is often considered rule number one for investors. You already know this intuitively. If you are hosting a dinner party but don't know your guests' dietary restrictions, it would be in your best interest to have as diverse a menu as possible. The more food options available, the more likely everybody will find something to eat.

This intuition seems to break down for our careers. We are largely encouraged to specialize, but, like the ice-cream and hot chocolate vendors, we work in roles and industries that are influenced by forces that are much bigger than any one person. In our cases it's probably not the weather dictating our business—though it might be. Rather, the forces are more likely to be things like technology innovation, globalization, financial markets, and sometimes a factor as simple as a virus. Concentrating our careers on one job at a time can be a risky move. It leaves us vulnerable to fluctuations in the market, the industry, our company, and our teams.

A freelance mindset, in which you work simultaneously for multiple employers or even industries, offers both an opportunity and a hedge. It allows you to cultivate new skills and gain exposure to new industries so that if one industry starts to decline, you have already been retrained for a new job. On the flip side, if one industry really takes off, you have a point of entry, but also have a hedge if the growth turns out to be short-lived.

Rather than viewing your career narrowly as a sequence of jobs at individual employers, you can create a basket of skills, interests, and clients that you look to holistically as one portfolio that grows over time. This concept of *portfolio careers* was introduced by Charles Handy in *The Age of Unreason* and is becoming more popular now in the age of freelancing.[11]

WORKING THROUGH YOUR FEARS TO DO WHAT YOU LOVE

The trouble with *Tick, Tick . . . BOOM!* is that it sets up a false dichotomy. It forces us to choose between all fear or all love, with nothing in between. In the world of freelancing, this sounds like a choice between only freelance or only one full-time job. The beauty of the freelance mindset, however, is that it involves seeing past these false all-or-nothing choices we have been led to believe are our only options. You *can* choose more.

The freelance mindset may mean freelancing and having a job at the same time. Many repeat freelancers told me that the second time they went into freelancing, they were sure to have at least a part-time or full-time job to provide some structure and benefits if they needed it. Moreover, fear serves a purpose in our lives. It exists to help us stay safe. The trouble is when that fear goes unchecked and we give in to it without examining whether the fear is well-founded and can be managed. So let's do that now. Let's look at the different fears that might keep you from accepting the call to adventure and see how we can manage them.

Facing Financial Risks

If financial fears are holding you back from venturing into a freelancing career or if you are thinking about leaving freelancing because you're not earning enough, consider some ways to address these challenges. Can you:

- Get a full-time or part-time job to provide a steady paycheck?
- Find one or two clients for a longer project?
- Raise your rates?

- Double down on your most successful project so far?
- Work in an adjacent industry that might need your experience?
- Go back to a previous client or employer if you need to?

Preparing financially before you start freelancing is ideal if you can manage it, but sometimes circumstances don't allow for that. In chapter 5 we'll discuss ways to add multiple income streams to your freelance business plan so you can be less dependent on any one source.

Addressing Health Concerns

Lack of health insurance or affordable health care is a common fear for freelancers or would-be freelancers. Chapter 6 will discuss more concrete options for managing your health as a freelancer, but here are a few possibilities to explore. Can you:

- Buy your own health insurance policy?
- Join a union or a freelancers' community that provides insurance?
- Find a full-time job or long-term contracting job that provides benefits?
- Set up a health savings account?
- Buy disability insurance to guard against larger health expenses or even loss of income?

Whether you work full-time as a freelancer or not, you need to protect your health preventatively. Be as firm about your working hours as possible so that you have time to rest, exercise, and do whatever else it takes to maintain your physical and mental health. Remember that even as a freelancer, you can and should set your own boundaries to navigate your career in the most sustainable and fulfilling way possible.

Building Relationships

If you're concerned about isolation as a freelancer, or anxious about diving into a new industry where you lack relationships or expertise, first think about how you will manage relationships proactively with the people who will help you on your journey: your clients and your community.

If you are on a freelancing platform where one unhappy client can give you a low rating that future clients can see, taking good care to maintain the relationship will be a high priority so you will have an easier time getting clients when you need freelance work. If the client is difficult or unhappy, take a deep breath. Then handle it just as you would want your favorite restaurant to do if they mixed up your order: Apologize to your client, volunteer to redo any work that can realistically be redone, and offer a discount or even a full refund. You may also take the extra steps of showing how you will fix the problem by doing something differently or referring the client to a different freelancer or vendor who might be able to help. But be cautioned: Just like at restaurants, freelance clients may sometimes express disappointment in the hopes of getting a freebie. If you suspect your client is doing this and you have completed the work as they specified, stand your ground and ask the freelance platform to intervene if possible.

Most of your freelance interactions will be positive, and you can weather the few negative ones more easily if you have a strong community. Surrounding yourself with people you connect with is especially important when you're self-employed. Can you:

- Volunteer or work for free to gain experience and start building relationships in the new area you are trying to break into?
- Take courses or join mastermind groups to learn new skills while meeting others in your chosen industry?
- Meet people in your company or clients' companies doing the thing that interests you and help them with small tasks?

Finding your new tribe may seem daunting at first, but take heart. By listening to your sparks of curiosity and taking incremental steps in their direction, you will push open doors and find the companions you need for your journey into the unknown world of freelancing.

Cultivating Resilience

Developing strategies to manage these individual fears can build up to greater resilience over time. Psychiatrist and writer Divya Chhabra urges freelancers to realize that resilience is a skill you can improve, not something that is fixed at birth.

"Resilience is not something that's innate in people. That's a huge myth," she said.[12] While genetic and environmental factors can support resilience, there are concrete steps freelancers can take to grow their resilience and better navigate an uncertain career. Divya recommends preparing for your journey into freelancing the way you might prepare for any other trip: by packing the things you'll need in advance. She suggested the following example.

If you're a writer, in your metaphorical tool kit you might want someone to check in on you every day to see if you're writing. That can help you stay motivated. You will also want to try to have enough money saved or available through projects or grants to last you for a certain amount of time. This can help you feel safe. You might set up your workspace so it has your favorite books or tea. This can help you focus. If you can carve out a couple of hours a week for a ritual or routine that you do for yourself, like an exercise class, this can help you feel grounded when the rest of your schedule is unpredictable, as well as help keep you healthy. Together these components can increase our resilience and our ability to navigate the challenges that life—whether freelance or otherwise—can throw our way.

You have been called to a great adventure, but only you can decide how to answer the call. Since you are reading this book right now, deep down you might know what you already want to do. But how do you pursue your career while navigating the very real fears of failure?

This is one of the most powerful aspects of the freelance mindset: using your fear to help you pursue your love. As my dad and countless other wise people would say, we need to plan for the worst and hope for the best. Successful freelancers learn how to perform this balancing act. They practice it week after week, month after month. But most importantly, when the call comes, they say yes.

SUMMARY

- Deciding how to incorporate freelancing into your life depends on a realistic assessment of the risks of *both* freelance work and full-time employment.
- Use freelancing to manage your financial risks by working for combinations of different clients, in different industries, or using different skill sets at the same time.
- Successful freelancers prioritize building strong support systems.

3

MAKING THE LEAP

It was the summer of 1968 when Finis Jhung sat in the Place du Casino in Monte Carlo contemplating his life. Thirty-one years old and a principal dancer in the Harkness Ballet, Finis was at the peak of his career. He had risen from poverty to become one of ballet's most sought-after dancers on stage and in Hollywood. But something was missing. Finis gazed at the looming old building from which the heroine in the famous ballet film *The Red Shoes* plunged to her death. He realized the time had come for him to do the same—metaphorically, at least.[1]

Finis had begun practicing Buddhism two years prior and found that it transformed his life and positively impacted those around him in a way that performing ballet could not. He decided to devote himself to Buddhism full-time. In the spring of 1969 Finis gave notice to his astonished director, flew back to New York City, and promptly got a nine-to-five job as a typist for a private investor. There he spent his days in the office and his nights and weekends volunteering with his Buddhist group. Despite the reputation of traditional employment as lucrative and stable, his typing job was a big pay cut from his salary as a company dancer. Finis accordingly downsized his life, but it was not enough. He struggled to make ends meet before finding himself in dire straits when the company abruptly shut down. Once again, Finis was looking for work.

With no idea what to do or where to go, he asked his Buddhist leader, Kenji Sudo, for advice. Kenji responded, "Teach ballet."[2]

Finis scrambled to relearn the ballet steps and technique he had forgotten during his two-year stint in the corporate world. His next challenge was to find students to teach. This proved tougher than he had anticipated. His first class had only four students.

Today he is celebrating more than fifty years of freelancing as a ballet teacher and video and music producer. His sales have grossed more than $6 million in the last twenty-seven years, and he has taught everyone from dance superstars to thousands of adult beginners around the world (including the hopelessly un-balletic yours truly).

His story is remarkable, but it illustrates several lessons for emerging freelancers. When you accept the call to embark on a freelance adventure, you leap from your familiar world and enter a brand-new paradigm of what work and life can be.

Freelancing may be a riskier path in some ways, as discussed in the previous chapter, but leaning into the uncertainty can help us build more meaningful lives over time. Like any complex or unfamiliar dance, let's break down this leap into the unknown, step by step.

WHERE ARE YOU GOING?

Ah, yes, the dreaded interview question. "Where do you see yourself in five years?" Freelancing gives you the opportunity to craft a new, more personal answer than ever before. Perhaps you know directionally where you want to go, but not how to get there. Freelance film director Alex Smith dreamed of directing movies, but so far he had only been hired to direct advertisements full-time.[3] Through freelancing, Alex got to do more creatively satisfying work, even though that sometimes involved directing student films for free. Or, perhaps, you're still exploring what you'd like to do next. A new career path may be emerging beneath your feet and you are still unsure where it can go—and where you would like it to go. That's an exciting stage in the journey.

We may be accepting the call to an adventurous new way of working, but we are also creating a way of life that will unfold over the coming days, months, and years. The long-term horizon means your first leap into freelancing doesn't have to be massive—and probably shouldn't be. I spoke with leadership coach Kristan Sargeant to learn more.

"Most people can't afford to just change their lives wholesale," she explained.[4] Her clients, like most of us, have personal responsibilities, years of work or school experience, and some level of purpose in their existing careers. But they come to her when they feel stuck in the lives they have created, as if something is missing.

The remedy she suggests is to get really curious about the sense of stagnation leading you to make a change. What parts of yourself aren't fully satisfied or expressed? When do you feel most excited or energized during your day? Chances are, your answers will be subtle at first. You may only get "a little clue, like a tiny bread crumb," she said. That's okay. We may have hidden or ignored these parts of ourselves for years. It will take time for us to learn how to bring them into the light.

When we get a spark of an answer, it's best to start moving. "We start taking action in the direction of that hunch," she said. This step may be as small as speaking up if the barista gets our coffee order wrong or as big as going back to school to learn a new trade. In our freelance journey, the important thing is to take a step toward the direction that feels authentic to us. If we're not feeling satisfied in our job, we don't have to quit. But we should listen to what is missing and try to incorporate bite-sized aspects of it into our daily life.

One example is an emergency room doctor Kristan coached. To treat his feelings of stagnation, he started writing down his sparks of interest and curiosity throughout the day. These shifts could be small, like having coffee with someone from a different industry, jotting down ideas for a side project, or even changing up the music and podcasts on his playlists. Yet they gave him a newfound sense of excitement and allowed him to be more present during his workday. He now finds meaning in both a job well done *and* collecting moments that keep his inspiration alive. Kristan told me, "He's discovering more space within his life to be more satisfied and fulfilled, and it hasn't meant leaving his job."

Those tiny movements can create dramatic shifts in our lives. Just like dancers train their muscles and technique on smaller jumps before making grand leaps, the incremental changes you make now can prepare you to really take flight later. For Erin Levi, a freelance travel and food writer, preparation looked like first writing about restaurants in New York City, where she lived, while also maintaining a full-time job in public relations.[5] Eventually, when her portfolio and network were strong enough, she took a leap into freelance writing full-time and has since been hired to write about more distant places, including Bhutan, Uzbekistan, Thailand, Nepal, and the Caribbean. Whether you eventually change careers, add another one, or dive deeper into a hobby is up to you.

Such change doesn't come easily. Even if it's a small action, "it will feel risky," Kristan cautions. "Anytime we digress even just a millimeter away from the pack, it feels really scary." But it's worth doing because action feeds both insights and further change. When we are trying to blaze a new trail for ourselves, the key is to start small and to keep moving forward.

Once we have a direction, it's only natural to want to have a destination. Even though the five-year-plan question in an interview feels a bit artificial, it raises the important question of what comes next.

My interviews with freelancers reveal that it's good to make plans but better to hold them loosely. Very few people had an explicit outcome they were working toward. Many people had this flexible outlook partly because freelancing emerged as an unexpected solution to a different career challenge.

One group, disenchanted with their career trajectory, decided to take agency into their own hands and change course. Moira MacDonald was a reporter working full-time for a newspaper in Toronto. With a journalist's eye, she observed the reporters and editors ahead of her. "I was seeing people who looked pretty burned out and not very happy," she said. "And I thought to myself, that's not going to be me."[6] Moira pitched multiple magazines and lined up some freelance writing assignments before leaving her job. Then she flew to New Zealand to write her first freelance assignment, beginning what turned into a twenty-year freelance journey. This giant career shift unfolded for Moira through a series of smaller movements away from a future she knew wasn't right for her.

Others took small steps toward an enticing opportunity that then added up to a bigger shift. Matthew Huff was working full-time at a literary agency when he unexpectedly got a book deal.[7] Initially he was asked to help an author with her book proposal, but he was eventually promoted to ghostwriter, then coauthor, and finally sole author of a book on marathons when the original writer became too busy with work to complete the draft. For Mathew and others like him, freelancing on side projects is a way to gain exposure in a new area without upending their established careers until they are ready to make a larger change.

Not everyone gets to practice before a big leap. Sometimes the decision is made for us and we have to adapt. Each year millions start freelancing because they were let go or couldn't find traditional full-time employment quickly enough, especially in a weak economy. As John Kador, a writer whose freelance career began when he was fired from a job, told me, "I got sick of getting fired, so I figured the only way to guarantee that I would never get fired is if I work for myself. So far, it's worked." He has been a full-time freelancer now for more than thirty years.

The beauty of the freelance mindset lies in being open to possibilities. Freelancing would not have emerged as an option for most people if they had clutched their five-year plans and refused to change with new information.

WHAT DO YOU NEED?

Before you make this career leap, you'll need a few tools. In the old way of working and living, you picked a goal and set your sights tenaciously on it for the remainder of your career. For a freelance mindset, you'll need a different skill set: awareness, flexibility, and perspective.

Awareness

To make career and life decisions well, you'll need to be paying attention. To what? First, to yourself. Everybody's method for tuning into themselves may be different, but you'll need to have some sort of practice for reflection. For Moira, this practice meant looking at her coworkers and paying attention to how the thought of living that life in the future made her feel. For the emergency room doctor, it meant paying attention to his daily routine and noticing when he felt stuck and when he felt inspired and then making small tweaks to bring more of the inspired moments into his day.

Between the back-to-back meetings and relentless flurry of emails, we often lose touch with how we actually feel in any given moment, because we are so focused on crossing off the next item on our to-do lists. Kristan recommends that everyone find a way to cultivate this present-moment awareness. What this looks like is deeply personal—after all, it needs to make *you* pay attention—but some examples of practices that can work well include journaling, meditation, prayer, yoga, running, and even extreme sports. Choose an activity that makes you feel present and that you can make time for at least once a week. Set an intention or give yourself a question to reflect on before starting your practice, and then see what comes up for you.

Once we have an inner awareness of how we are responding to the stimuli in our lives, we can turn that awareness outward to see how the world is changing around us. In her book *Flux*, futurist April Rinne reminds us that what we actually see in any given situation is limited by our social and cultural orientation.[8] In one example, people from individualist and collectivist cultures looked at the same picture. The individualists' eyes were drawn to the foreground of the picture, while the collectivists were more likely to look at the background and environment.[9] Both groups looked at the same picture, and yet both saw different things. When it comes to our careers, what opportunities and threats do we see? Shifting to a freelance mindset means recognizing our worldview may be narrower than we realize. We need to zoom out from a very limited image of a career path to discover the full range of possibilities and unexpected combinations that exist, hiding in plain sight for us to find them.

Presence

Many freelancers described a real urgency to the way they lived their lives. On a larger scale, the pandemic may have been a turning point, reducing our tolerance for deferred dreams. A study by the American Psychological Association found that about half of Americans felt it was impossible to plan for the future because of the coronavirus pandemic.[10] At the same time, more than three in five respondents (61 percent) believed the pandemic made them rethink how they were living their lives.[11] People became more aware of their mortality amid the staggering collective loss. This increased awareness of mortality made people less willing to delay gratification indefinitely.

"I have never experienced people so hungry to ask the deeper questions around what will satisfy them. And then have the patience and tolerance to live in the ambiguity that comes with asking these kinds of questions," Kristan told me.

In Buddhism—which Finis practiced—as in many Western traditions, like Stoicism, people are encouraged to face their own mortality on a regular basis.[12] By recognizing that our time is finite, we can live more courageously today. A simple practice to boost your awareness may involve meditating on the fact that everyone will die, including us. One meditation teacher encourages each of his students to stand up and say a sentence like, "My name is Maya Roy. I was born on January 5, 1990. I grew up in San Francisco, California. I, too, will die."[13] Or the practice may become as involved as visiting a charnel ground, cemetery, or crematorium to ponder the fact that one day your body will also come to rest here.[14] While it may sound morbid, the end result is meant to be liberating. By coming to terms with the temporary nature of our lives, we can live fearlessly today.

Flexibility

When we start to shift our attention to the present, we may start to notice just how little is actually under our control. Whether you want to call it randomness, luck, or fate, many freelancers mentioned how pure chance had shaped their careers. For some, it was a chance encounter with somebody they hadn't met in years—if ever.

Finis recounts the most challenging part of his career.[15] It was in 1987, when he shuttered the dance company he founded after sinking most of his life savings into it. He wandered the streets of Manhattan, posting flyers to advertise his dance classes, but not enough students turned up to cover the cost of rent and real estate taxes. He decided to leave the city, and applied to teach dance in his home state of Hawaii—but was rejected. Just on the verge of giving up, he got a surprise phone call from a stranger named Richard Ellner. Richard owned Broadway Dance Center (BDC), which is now an iconic dance studio in Hell's Kitchen. Richard asked if Finis would come teach for him. In exchange, Richard would take over the struggling Finis Jhung Ballet Studio. Finis would get paid for every student that attended his classes, and have no expenses. He describes it as nothing short of a miracle.

Several freelancers recalled having similar experiences.[16] A client needed some work done and had heard of this freelancer through some mysterious grapevine. The client made a chance phone call to the freelancer and the rest was history. These calls sometimes turned into long working relationships that were both professionally and financially rewarding. Such good fortune can appear if you are actively searching for it, or at least open to the possibility of it arriving.

Flexibility is an essential ingredient of the freelance mindset. What makes freelancers special is the way they respond to uncertainty: not by shrinking away but by facing it head-on. This approach allows them to nimbly respond to market changes. For many freelance writers I interviewed, their awareness allowed them to observe trends in what their clients wanted. Flexibility allowed them to change their workload to seize those opportunities. For example, some changed from writing articles to writing corporate annual reports and, later, to ghostwriting books as both the market demand and their skill sets evolved. Their trade was writing throughout their freelance careers, but they managed to repurpose what they wrote to match the needs of the day. This openness to change means we can pounce on new jobs as they are created, since there is always the possibility that our next—or best—job may not even exist yet.

TIME TO LEAP

A short ballet lesson may be especially instructive for thinking about your leap into a freelance life. I asked Finis what makes some dancers leap better than others. Why did Mikhail Baryshnikov defy gravity when others (ahem, including me) barely leave the ground?

The answer comes down to three things: preparation, focus, and timing. Even the most talented dancers must also take care to get these things right. It turns out that these critical aspects of ballet technique are also remarkably instructive for workers thinking about leaping into the unknown of freelancing. Let's explore the similarities now.

Preparation

"That's the only way you can jump," Finis told me. "Prepare."[17]

When he coaches ballet dancers to leap, preparation looks like lining up their bodies correctly then pushing their feet against the floor as hard as they can, from the heel to the ball to the toe. For workers leaping into the world of freelance, preparation also starts at your foundation.

You can only take flight if you feel supported. How can you support yourself financially, physically, emotionally, and otherwise? Knowing you have a plan to handle these basics can allow you to shift your attention elsewhere. We covered the risks and how you can prepare for them in the previous chapter, but at a high level, preparing to leap means you have done the work and put a plan in place—and you trust yourself to figure things out if the world changes around you. This might mean answering questions like these: Do I have a safety net from savings or a job? Do I have health insurance or an equivalent? Do I have any paying or free clients lined up? Do I have credentials from past work or classes to demonstrate my skill set? Do I have friends and mentors I can talk to when I feel stuck? Do I know what makes me feel calm? Once you gather this information, you're ready to move to the next stage of your leap.

Focus

Where you look is almost as important as what your feet do.

"The bigger the jump, the higher you look," Finis said. "That's what all good dancers do. You can't jump looking at the floor."

For a freelancer, this means that, of all the possible options, you need to select where to focus your attention. Now that you have prepared, you don't need to look down to see how far you can fall. You also don't have to look left and right, by comparing yourself to your peer group. Your friends might be buying a second home while you're living with roommates. Or maybe they just don't understand your career decisions.

Freelance content creator and writer Paul Millerd notes that one of the biggest challenges of leaving a traditional employment path is navigating other people's reactions. "People will ask, 'Why are you doing this? What's your plan?'" If this barrage of curiosity tempts you to question yourself, hold strong. "These things can throw you into mini existential crises," he said. "Having the capacity to be able to deal with that is way more important than people imagine." The gift of freelancing is getting to create a career and life that is authentic to your values. That kind of life is worth fighting for.

So pay little attention to the naysayers, the hecklers, or that one person loudly munching popcorn even though there are signs everywhere saying it's not allowed in the theater (hypothetically speaking, of course). If you get distracted by what everyone else is doing, your own leap will not be able to reach its full potential. Decide what you're aiming for—maybe it's more income, more creative fulfillment, or more autonomy. Then set your sights high, and allow your entire being to move toward that goal.

Timing

All the technique in the world can't help you if you don't leap on the right count. Even a split second can make all the difference. Early in his career, Finis danced the *Grand Pas Espagnol*. The choreography was beautiful, but Finis wasn't jumping high enough in rehearsal. He practiced intensely in the days leading up to the show. During the performance, Finis leaped with all his might. When the newspaper reviewed the piece, it included a photo of this jump that showed Finis soaring high above the other dancers.

"Of course," he laughs, "there was another explanation. It could be that I jumped later than the other two."[18]

For freelancers, our careers are not choreographed. Unlike in a ballet performance, you can't actually be late for a leap into freelancing. You can prepare for as long as you'd like, but preparing endlessly for scenarios that may not come to pass is usually fear (aka emotional gravity) trying to keep us in our place. You have to actually jump to become airborne. So if there's something new you want to add to your career and you have a chance, consider this your sign to go for it. And if the decision to freelance was made for you—perhaps because you were laid off—the time is now. Let's leap!

Freelance transitions may sometimes seem dramatic, especially if you are leaving a stable job or industry in order to start something new. However, leaning into this uncertainty can help you live more fearlessly and pursue more meaning in all aspects of your life. Before you can leap into a new way of working, it is important to understand in which direction you want to go. Reflection is essential for freelancers. A deep understanding of your interests and motivations helps you recognize—and pounce on—enticing new opportunities when they appear. And when these opportunities do appear, with nimble preparation, high aim, and timely action you, too, can soar like a ballet master toward your dreams.

SUMMARY

- Advance your freelance journey by paying attention to your curiosity and courageously taking small steps in the directions that excite you.
- Acknowledging how much of our lives are out of our control prompts us to take the risks in our personal and professional lives that matter most to us.
- Manage the uncertainty of a freelance career by doing as much preparation as possible before diving into it full-time.

II

NAVIGATING THE TRAIL

4

UNCOVERING YOUR SPECIALTY

On November 9, 2019, hundreds of twenty- and thirtysomethings decked out in their most fashionable clothes, makeup, and jewelry headed to the trendy neighborhood of Chelsea in New York City for the event of the season. Was it a nightclub? No. It was seven-thirty on a Saturday morning, and this excited crowd was waiting to attend the second annual Slashie Summit.

Hosted by *Brown Girl Magazine* the Slashie Summit is described as "a collaborative and immersive experience that empowers hustlers, doers, and creators to uncover their purpose and achieve financial independence despite the stigma behind creative aspirations."[1] Attendees proudly displayed the many slashes on their name tags as indications of their multiple professional hats. For example, in attendance were Vyjayanthi, the anthropologist/actor, and Darsh, the actor/model/engineer, both of whom have had successful careers as full-time freelancers. Some attendees at the early stage of exploring their interests expressed difficulty choosing which slashes to display. Excitement sometimes turned to feeling overwhelmed as they wondered how accomplished they had to be before announcing their slashes to the world. I struggled with this too. Did wanting to write a book make me a writer? I decided yes, and added it to my name tag.

The Slashie Summit (also called "Slashie") was a breakthrough place for South Asian creatives to authentically express the full breadth of their interests and capabilities and find interesting collaborators. Slashie has since become a flagship event and community for the *Brown Girl Magazine* brand, where I have previously freelanced. Friendships blossomed from the single-day event, resulting in creative collaborations like writing projects, short films, dances, and consulting engagements. Now these opportunities to collaborate also exist through ongoing virtual meetups and webinars.

In the last few years, many names have popped up to describe this multi-career or multi-interest lifestyle. But the question remains: Is it wise to have multiple professional identities? After all, who hasn't heard the saying "Jack of all trades, master of none"? The saying is catchy, but is it accurate? What if having more than one area of focus could make you better at everything you do? An emerging body of research suggests this might be the case. Let's explore.

GENERALIST, SPECIALIST, OR SOMETHING ELSE?

When you tell people you're a freelancer, their natural reaction (if they're polite) is to ask what kind of freelancing you do. How do you decide what sort of freelancing you want to do? Seasoned freelancers will tell you to figure out which of your capabilities or interests distinguishes you from everybody else. This distinction is your specialty. But where does this line of thinking lead you? Does it mean you only have to do one thing forever and that's it?

Psychologist Sarabeth Berk studies professional identity. She argues that there are three types of professional identity people can have: singularity, multiplicity, and hybridity.[2]

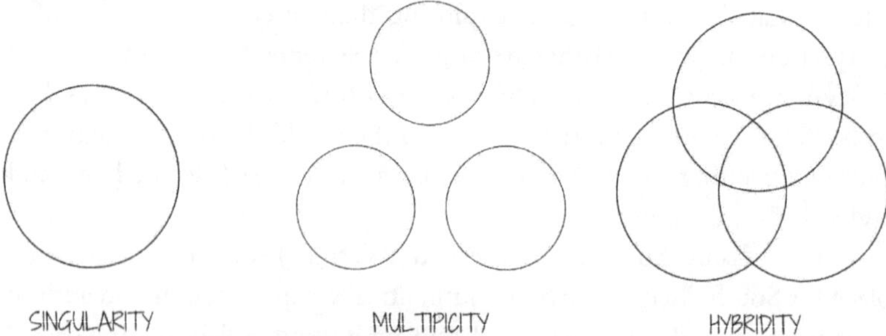

Figure 4.1. Types of Professional Identities. *Source*: Illustration by Tanaya Raj

Singularity means you only possess one professional identity. You're not a jack- or jill-of-all-trades. For instance, maybe you only see yourself as a writer. Even though you might write differently in different styles—say, articles, books, and marketing materials—the idea of being more than a writer (like being a strategist or a designer) doesn't appeal to you. In that case, you have a single professional identity as a writer.

Multiplicity means you have two or more professional identities, but you keep them separated, consciously or unconsciously. One of my classmates became a lawyer and a dancer. It is very hard to practice law while dancing, and very hard to dance while practicing law. These are clearly different professional hats, and she only wears one at any time, but both are incredibly important to her.

The final category is hybridity, a twist on multiplicity. People with hybrid professional identities have multiple professional identities but instead of separating them, they work in the space where all their identities intersect. Sarabeth's primary professional identities are artist, researcher, educator, and designer. Together, they intersect to make Sarabeth what she describes as a "creative disruptor." She draws on the skills from each of her domains simultaneously. Sarabeth explains that multiplicity is like having flour, water, sugar, and eggs sitting separately on your counter as ingredients. You can keep them separate. Or you can mix them together and form something new, which becomes a hybrid combination. When the ingredients are baked together, they transform from their original state into something else entirely: a delicious cake.[3]

It's tempting to think that because hybridity is like going from many parts to being a cake, it must somehow be better than the other forms of professional identities. That's not the case. Whether your professional identity is singular, multiple, or hybrid, the important thing is to figure out which form applies to you at this moment and then double down on it. The result might be that you have a single specialty that others recognize, you have multiple specialties, or you create a new specialty that is entirely unique to you (which Sarabeth likes to call your "hybrid expertise"). Deciding which identity is the best fit for you today depends on an honest inventory of your skills and interests, as well as the market. That's the best way to build a career you find both satisfying and sustainable.

After reading this, you can probably also think of aspects of your life that you love (like working out or cooking) and that are very much a part of your personal identity but have never been part of your professional identity. Should they be? When we can have multiple or overlapping professional identities, which aspects of our lives should we make professional and which, if any, should stay truly personal? In other words, should we monetize our joy?

SHOULD YOU MONETIZE YOUR JOY?

The question of whether to monetize your joy assumes that you know what brings you joy. You might know, or you might have been so busy with work and life that you haven't reflected on the question recently. If that's the case, a great place to start is by observing yourself throughout the day and paying attention to when you feel most energized and excited. Flow, or the state of being so absorbed in what you are doing that you lose track of time and your activity seems almost effortless, is one quality to notice if you experience it at any point in your day.[4] If you don't necessarily feel flow, the next approach would be curiosity. Julia Cameron, author of *The Artist's Way*, suggests carving out one hour a week to devote to just following your curiosity and doing things that spark your interest or seem like they would be fun, without expecting anything from that time.[5] Journaling, reflection, and guided visualization are also useful tools.[6] At this early stage, coach Kristan Sargeant reminds us, the goal isn't necessarily to find your definitive joy but to hunt for clues that could lead you closer to it.[7]

To tackle this question of monetizing your joy—which, by the way, has extremely personal answers—it can be useful to think of your purpose as the intersection of yourself and the world. One framework, which is sometimes mapped to your life's purpose or the Japanese concept of *ikigai* ("reason for being"), shows four overlapping circles: (1) what you enjoy, (2) what you're good at, (3) what the world needs, and (4) what you can get paid for. The center of the diagram, where all these circles intersect, is the ultimate sweet spot, signifying your purpose, or *ikigai*.[8] Some people say this sweet spot represents your purpose for being alive. But this interpretation might be a little dramatic. If you can

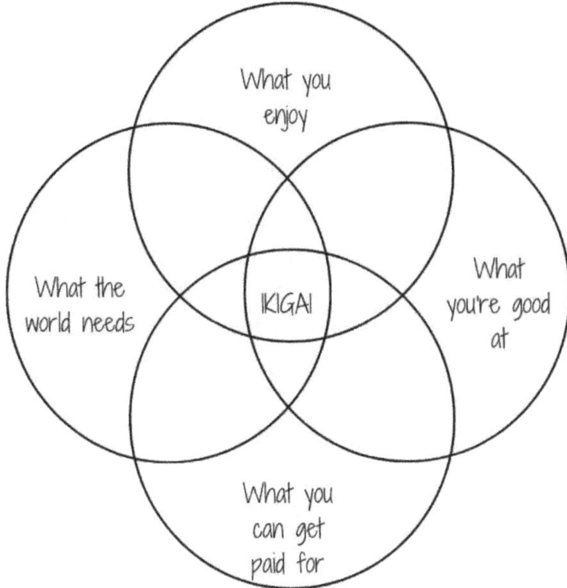

Figure 4.2. *Ikigai* Circles. *Source*: Illustration by Tanaya Raj

find that place and make money doing things you love and are good at, and the world wants them and will pay for them, that's fantastic! By all means, *please* do that. But many of us are still looking for that special zone of genius. We might feel fragmented, or we might only fill a couple of circles at any given time. For us, the question is whether we should take what we love doing and try to nudge it closer to what we can get paid for.

The answer is tricky, because our 24/7 hustle culture wants us to monetize everything we do. We've all heard the saying "Do what you love, and you'll never work a day in your life." That is, at best, a fairly unhelpful exaggeration. Variations of this advice may be why many people turn their hobbies into side hustles even when they generate very little income, instead of just enjoying the activities for their own sake. The question is especially tricky for freelancers, because spending time on activities we don't get paid for can mean not spending that same time on another activity we *would* get paid for.

As you start thinking about whether to put your passion into your business plan, it can be helpful to reflect on what motivates you. The first question is where you are in your financial and personal journey. Psychologist Abraham Maslow's well-known theory on the hierarchy of needs (often called "Maslow's hierarchy of needs") is a useful framework to describe the way we prioritize our different needs as human beings. Maslow's hierarchy of needs is usually drawn as a pyramid that shows we first satisfy our needs for physical well-being, safety, love and belonging, and esteem, in that order.[9] Once all the needs below the very top of the pyramid are met, we can focus on *self-actualization*, or, our purpose.

Importantly, for every need before self-actualization, our motivation to keep building those areas of our lives decreases as the needs are met. This makes sense; if we are really hungry, we will consider finding food extremely urgent. Once our belly is full, we can spend our energy on solving different problems, like whether we are in the right job.

Another way of thinking about monetizing your passions is whether your motivation is extrinsic or intrinsic. Extrinsic motivation means you're motivated by something external to you—like money. Intrinsic motivation is internal; it could be things like enjoyment or mastery. Since we are talking about something you already enjoy doing, we can assume you're intrinsically motivated. You're doing it because you want to. So if you could get paid for that (and have some extrinsic motivation), wouldn't that be better?

A classic psychology study put this question to the test. In the early 1970s, Edward Deci studied college students doing things they were already intrinsically motivated to do, like solving puzzles and writing newspaper headlines. He and his colleagues experimented with what happened if some of these students were paid for how many puzzles they solved or headlines they wrote. The payments were small, just $1 per puzzle and $0.50 per newspaper headline. In today's dollars, this would be roughly $7 a puzzle and $3.50 for each newspaper headline.[10] Once students started getting paid for things they enjoyed doing, their intrinsic motivation to do those things dropped. They were still motivated to do them, but they were more motivated by the money. On the flip side, when there was no money involved but the students got a different kind of extrinsic motivation—praise—their intrinsic motivation stayed the same.[11]

What might Deci's findings mean for your own work? First, your relationship to what you love could change after doing it professionally.

Shalene Gupta, who grew up without a TV at home, absolutely loved to read as a child. Now she is a freelance writer. "It's not relaxing to read anymore," she said.[12] She starts analyzing what worked and what didn't in each story she reads. "It's become like market research," she said. Now when she wants to relax, she doesn't read contemporary novels or nonfiction like she used to before becoming a professional in those genres. Instead she started reading 1800s Victorian novels, because they are so far removed from what is happening in the industry today.

Something similar happened to me when I went to India to act. Watching Bollywood movies had long been an escape for me. Once I started auditioning for them, I couldn't watch them in the same way I once did. Movies stopped being fanciful, and I started analyzing everything about them from the acting to the script and, yes, of course, the casting decisions. Now I watch different genres to relax. (Hello, K-drama!)

Second, when you try to monetize your joy, the work you can be paid for might still not be the work you crave doing. Most seemingly "joyful" professions are still highly competitive. In the movie *Black Swan*, the best ballet dancer in the company finds her mental health rapidly deteriorating as she tries to get—and then keep—her role as a principal dancer in her company. But the alternative is equally challenging. If you've seen *Center Stage*, Jodie worries that she'll spend her "best dancing years in the back of a corps [de ballet] waving a rose back and forth" because she was unlikely to get selected as a principal dancer.[13] It's hard to make it to the top, even if you are very, very good. And even if you do make it to the top in terms of skill, there is no guarantee that what you find artistically fulfilling will be commercially successful. Even artists like Vincent van Gogh spent an entire lifetime toiling away without the art world caring. Van Gogh's work only became wildly successful *after* he died.[14]

If you are faced with the decision between doing work that is not as personally fulfilling but is still related to what brings you joy, you'll need to reflect on whether the work is still worth doing. In these moments, Magaly Colimon-Christopher, an actor on the Netflix series *Grand Army*, always asks herself this question: "Does this feed me artistically, or does it feed me as a human being, or do I need to just eat? And choosing one or the other . . . it's personal. There's no right or wrong answer to that."[15] There are trade-offs each time you decide to keep your joy pure or stay true to your art. "If you do go for the artistic choice and say no [to work] because it doesn't feed you spiritually," Magaly said, "you know the consequences you're going to pay will be doing a job that helps you survive and eat in order to wait for that moment when you're going to be fed artistically." And that job might be in this industry or another one entirely. That's for you to choose.

Even with these trade-offs, many people go for it anyway and decide to monetize their passions. For Shalene, it was a no-brainer to make writing her profession. "Maybe it's because I come from an immigrant background and I'm deeply practical and risk-averse, but I believe in monetizing your joy," she said. Magaly told me she had spent many years trying to convince herself she'd be happy doing something other than acting. She worked in insurance, then as a teacher, an arts administrator, and a skin-care entrepreneur, and took on many other roles along the way. Finally, she realized, "I had to admit I love my art form and doing anything else always feels like an aberration. Because whenever I get an audition, nothing matters but my audition." And for me, turning acting into a (brief) career felt similar. I knew I almost certainly wouldn't become a Bollywood star, but I couldn't live without exploring how that world worked.

HOW GOOD DO YOU HAVE TO BE?

With the many pressures that come from monetizing your joy, it's perfectly understandable why some people choose not to do it. They can keep their joy sacred by shielding it from outside demands. But what happens when the choice is made for you? Let's say you would monetize your joy if you could; but, frankly, you're not that good at the activity that brings you joy. Let's explore why committing to your pursuit anyway might be a really wonderful thing, assuming you're not putting yourself at financial risk by doing so.

As a norm, our culture encourages children to try as many different extracurricular activities as they like. We give children a lot of grace for participating in activities, even if they're not that good at them. Accidentally scored a goal on your own team in the youth soccer game? Have an orange slice! (I may or may not be speaking from personal experience on that one.) Trip over your own feet and fall down during your dance recital? Oopsies! (Also speaking from personal experience—more than once—on that one.) We encourage children in this way because we know they are still growing. Their skills might improve. Or they might not. But even if the child is a terrible soccer player, we acknowledge that the kid can still make friends, get exercise, learn to be a team player, and have a good time—outcomes that are inherently worthwhile.

Somewhere around high school, so-called extracurriculars become really important. They play a large role in the college admissions process. So we start thinking that college is a proxy for your future ability to feed yourself and have shelter. And if extracurriculars are gatekeepers for college, your outside accomplishments today determine how likely you are even to *survive* in the future. Yikes! What happened to fun? This period, around the transition from high school to college, seems to be when many of us stop doing things simply for the sheer enjoyment of doing them.[16]

Now, as an adult, an age at which you are actively trying to feed yourself and keep a roof over your head, it feels almost rebellious to pursue an activity if you know you'll never do it professionally. The situation is especially fraught when you are a freelancer. If you are lucky to have work now, and don't know when it will dry up, you might feel pressure to monetize every possible hour of your time. When Matthew Huff first started freelancing, he thought, "I need to take everything that people are sending me. I need to write, like, all hours of the day and night so that I can get this money in."[17] Over time, he came to a realization: "Maybe I don't need to do this. I can sort of scale back. But there is a weird sort of guilt that comes when you're a freelancer. . . . You can always be working more, and you can always be making more money or making more connections."

Our society has a strained relationship with leisure time. The root of this tension, according to author and history professor Steven Gelber, is that our time can be spent in one of two ways: work or leisure.[18] At its best, Gelber notes, leisure can be synonymous with freedom, because you can only experience leisure while you are not working. But for that very same reason, leisure also signifies time wasted and earnings forgone.

As the pressures from capitalism grow, so does the tension between these two activities.

Coming back to the *ikigai* circles, if what you love doing is not what you can get paid for (maybe because it's not what the world needs or because it's not what you're good at), when is it still worth doing? In my opinion, always. Always, as long as it doesn't jeopardize your ability to take care of yourself with food, shelter, health care, and whatever else you need to survive. All sorts of benefits come from doing things we don't monetize or are actively bad at. We learn grit, resilience, humility, or another new skill. We get a fresh perspective of the problems we face in our working lives and new tools to solve those problems. We become more creative.[19] We make friends in different social circles (which often leads to more work).[20] And we can show up more fully in the rest of our lives because of these experiences. All these benefits make life fuller and more meaningful.

At least this is how I rationalize *still* taking dance classes, even though I may never conquer a double pirouette on purpose. My lifetime earnings from dance would probably not be enough to pay for a single dance class, never mind afford a cup of coffee afterward. Still, I don't want to imagine my life without dance. There is no minimum skill level needed or revenue generated to be worthy of experiencing delight. So, if you have any room in your life portfolio—in between paying your bills, seeing your friends, and staying healthy—to carve out time for whatever brings you joy, I urge you to please make space for it. Even if you feel silly or out of place. Especially so. Do it anyway. Nobody has to know but you.

SETTING YOUR BOUNDARIES

The beauty of the freelance mindset is that it puts you back at the center of your career and your life. It makes space for you to remember what brings you joy and then to discover how you'd like that joy to fit in your life. But, like anything else in life, our passions can be a source of delight or angst, depending on how we interact with them. Here are some ways to set boundaries with your passion so that you can have a fulfilling and ongoing relationship with it.

Take Breaks

It may seem counterintuitive, but knowing when to hit pause is essential, whether your passion is your livelihood or not. Often the impulse is to push through burnout. But sometimes you need breaks to protect your mind, your body, and your love of what you do.

During the coronavirus lockdown, I spent much of my free time taking virtual dance classes from teachers around the world. It was a chaotic year, and the tragedies were seemingly endless. Slowly the stress of the pandemic started taking a toll on my dance teachers as well. One by one, they stopped teaching. Some of them stopped dancing entirely. By late summer, every dance teacher I had studied with was on a break. They simply couldn't push themselves anymore. One teacher posted on Instagram that he had to stop dancing for a while in order to not hate dance.[21] Stopping can be incredibly difficult for dancers because they lose technique so quickly—within just a couple weeks of not training.[22] As freelance dance and figure skating teacher Inna Kuznetsova told me, "If you are a professional figure skater, you worked so hard to get the skill that now you have to just do it. It's like brushing your teeth."[23] And for freelancers in all industries, there is always the fear that your clients will move on. Taking a break can be frightening. Yet sometimes we have to take these breaks preventatively so that we can come back refreshed and have a long working life.

When it is time for a break, a few things can make that break more restorative and easier to come back from. First, communicate your break. Let your clients know that you are taking some time to reset and when you will be back. If you don't know how long you'll be gone, say you'll check back in after some common unit of time—next month, season, quarter, semester, or the like—and then do so. You may also want to post that you are taking a break on social media to keep future clients informed while you are away. (When you return, remember to reach out to your clients again so you can share why the break was useful and what you are excited to help them with next.) Second, think about how you would like to use your time. For some people, having a list of things to do each day feels satisfying. Even if the list just says, "catch up on sleep" and "cook dinner," it might offer the structure you crave. For others in the throes of burnout, lists are anathema. Decide which approach suits you best in this moment. Lastly, use some of the time to try an activity that is different from the one that burned you out. For my dance teachers who took breaks, this meant other active pursuits like yoga, hiking, or studying unfamiliar styles of dance. For me, when corporate work feels draining, I turn to the arts by acting, dancing, singing, or painting as a complete beginner.

Of course, if none of these catch your fancy, honor your own instincts of what your mind and body need. You are the authority on you.

Reevaluate Tasks

If a break is out of the question but certain tasks are more painful and less rewarding than others, see if you can renegotiate the work in your portfolio. One freelance writer used to transcribe interviews as a service but developed severe carpal tunnel syndrome that was interfering with the rest of her life. She eventually stopped doing transcriptions but expanded her other writing, editing, interviewing, and note-taking services. Are there tasks in your portfolio you can discontinue entirely? If not, can you subcontract to another freelancer who is open to doing them? Is there software available that could automate these parts of the work for you?

Find New Hobbies

If you decide to monetize something you used to do for fun, you might need to find new ways of having fun that aren't work. As she describes in her article in *Vox*, Marian Bull was a professional food writer whose therapist encouraged her to find a hobby.[24] She took up ceramics. This new pastime was exactly the physical and psychological outlet she craved. Marian shared her creations on social media—but then people asked to buy them. She agreed. Over time, ceramics turned into her main source of income (partly because she got laid off from her day job). While monetizing her hobby doesn't take the joy out of pottery for her, it adds a level of seriousness to it. Monetizing also adds other tasks, like marketing her work and maintaining a website, to her ceramic making. Along the way, Marian realized that ceramics had ceased to be her hobby, perhaps forever. She plans to continue it as a commercial endeavor, partly because of financial constraints, although it is one that she deeply enjoys. Marian now looks for new spaces in her life to find inspiration, relaxation, and peace of mind. Your hobbies may change too, and that's okay.

Say No

Ultimately, being at the whims of an industry can be too much to bear. Deciding to leave and to un-monetize your joy is a valid choice. Magaly, the actor mentioned earlier, told me, "I know a lot of people who left the industry because that imprecise approach to existing can be exhausting if you don't feed it with other endeavors and make it worth it. I respect them for saying no. It doesn't make them any less of an artist than someone who says yes and endures. They just say no to the pain."[25] You began exploring your hobbies because they felt good. If they are making you miserable and you are not able to shift the situation or your perspective adequately, the healthiest thing may just be to walk away. That might mean not doing this work for pay anymore, or it might mean closing the chapter on a certain side of yourself entirely. Both approaches are okay. We romanticize side hustles in our culture and idolize people who "make it" outside the confines of an office. But sometimes "making it" means having work be work and play be play, by carving out a few moments of time that are yours to just enjoy. You can shift your joy from job to side hustle to hobby to interest whenever the transition feels right to you.

Constantly Reassess

Know that what feels right for you today might be different from what feels right for you tomorrow. Sometimes that can be hard to accept because we become married to a version of ourselves, but we are always in a state of evolution. Magaly spoke about acting versus taking other work to pay the bills: "The balance of that scale, how much is about art and how much is about eating? Sometimes they're equal, sometimes one is higher than the other, and it vacillates. And it's not about the seasons of life. It's about the seasons of the *day*."[26] Check in with yourself often, and feel free to let your answers change.

As a freelancer, you have a unique opportunity to figure out what you want to do with your time and how you'd like to earn your living. To do this, you'll need to decide how many professional identities you'd like to have. Some people prefer to focus on a single area and become an expert. Others like to toggle between different, but separate, fields. And a third group likes to play where a few fields intersect. Discovering where along this spectrum you fall can help you work out how you spend your time. With that information, you can decide which aspects of your life you grant professional status and which ones, perhaps for your mental health or their integrity, remain personal. Having both professional and personal activities you care about is an essential tool that helps you navigate the highs and lows of life in the freelance world.

SUMMARY

- Consider how many aspects of your professional life you want to have as part of your identity. If there is more than one, are they separate identities, or do they intersect in an interesting way that makes you unique?
- Making time for things that bring you joy is important, but consider the skill level you need and how your relationship to your passions will change if you try to monetize them.
- Setting boundaries by taking breaks, performing different tasks, finding new hobbies, and saying no can help you cultivate a fulfilling and sustainable relationship with your passions.

5

CREATING YOUR BUSINESS PLAN

The movie *Band Baaja Baaraat* (released internationally as *Wedding Planners*) tells the story of Shruti Kakkar, a middle-class woman in Delhi on the verge of her college graduation. Shruti, played by Anushka Sharma, dreams of starting her own business. Shruti's parents want her to agree to an arranged marriage, which could mean the end of her career. She reaches a deal with her family: They give her five years to start her company. When she is twenty-five, she will get married, no matter what.

Shruti is determined to become the best wedding planner not just in Delhi but in all of India before her marriage. The only problem? She has no money, no connections, and just a very limited time to reach her goals.

I first watched this movie with a few friends during business school.[1] When it ended, we were struck by how well the movie illustrated the journey of start-up founders we had studied in class. Today, Shruti's story serves as a useful guide for freelancers as well. As we've seen, freelancing is fraught with uncertainty, but having a solid business plan can go a long way in helping you manage some of that risk.

DISCOVERING YOUR REASONS

An important piece of advice I received from former freelancers was this: Know why you are freelancing.[2] We talked earlier about the specific reasons we might freelance, but zooming out a bit, we can simplify our rationales for freelancing as to have either more money or more meaning. Both objectives are essential to a freelance mindset, but not every project can satisfy each reason equally. This chapter and the next will talk about financial objectives. Chapter 7 examines the drive to find meaning.

Even if you use freelancing primarily to satisfy your needs for fulfillment, thinking strategically about your income is essential. It will take some pressure off your creative pursuits and can give you peace of mind if you have some slow seasons of work. As freelance writer Shalene Gupta told me, "When I first quit my job to become a writer, I was willing to be dirt-poor. I thought money didn't matter and I just needed my art. Very quickly, I realized how easy it was to think I didn't need money when I had the luxury of a full-time salary. When that income is gone and you're living in an expensive city . . . yeah, you suddenly really care about money again."

You can go after work that will earn you more money today. Or you might invest time today in something that could bring you more money down the line—activities that, for example, might boost your expertise, add credentials to your professional identity, and build your network. Let's explore.

FINDING YOUR FIELD

The first step is picking your market. In the previous chapter we discuss how many professional identities you will have. Within each specialty, you will still have the question of what specific clients and markets to target. In *Band Baaja Baaraat*, Shruti carefully analyzes her options and selects an industry that she finds secure: wedding planning. She says that whether there is a recession or inflation, weddings will always happen.[3] Shruti clearly wants this business to grow into a reliable source of income. For your own reliable source of income, you'll need to do a similar analysis.

There are three aspects to consider at this point. First is the industry. Do you expect it to be stable regardless of the economic environment, like Shruti believes is true of wedding planning? How do you think the industry will evolve over time? A growing industry, as in the case of a new technology, may be more attractive but also more risky, since it has yet to reach its full potential. A declining industry is likely not the best choice for reliable income unless you believe the decline will be very slow, like over the course of decades. Next is the question of the work itself. Does it align with your skills or the skills you hope to gain? The final aspect to consider is how your specific offerings fit within this landscape. Do you have a lot of competition? If so, how can you make your offerings more unique so clients will have a reason to choose you over somebody else who could do a similar job?

Finally, are there different combinations of industries or companies you can explore that can reduce your overall risk, because one might succeed while the other declines, as we saw in chapter 2? For example, one dancer I interviewed freelances on the side for technology start-ups in their design departments. This kind of diversification helped her survive the pandemic when the performing arts shut down. She said, "Even though my whole industry went away, I was still able to make it work and keep at least my part-time job and have some kind of a safety net."[4] How concentrated are your offerings in any particular niche? Do you have at least two sectors so that, if one goes away, the other might tide you over?

WHAT ARE YOU CHASING?

Once you know which specific industries and clients you are focused on, the next step is to calibrate what you are working toward. A political strategy book by James Carville and Paul Begala talks about how important it is to set the right goals.[5] They tell the story of a lion in the wild. Lions are stronger and faster than every animal around them, from tiny rabbits to large antelopes. But if the lion spends all its time chasing rabbits, it will eventually wither away. This is because, as the authors write, the lion would spend more energy running after the rabbit than it gets back in sustenance. On this diet alone, the lion would starve. By contrast, if the lion pursues an antelope, achieving that goal would keep the lion full for a much longer period of time. The moral of Carville and Begala's story is that we should focus our energy on pursuing antelope goals wherever possible and leave the rabbits alone, because they are a distraction.

This is a helpful model, but for our freelancing savanna, I think we need to add a third type of goal that is even bigger: a giraffe. (Until I researched for this book, I hadn't realized that lions also sometimes chase giraffes—and it's a bit of a toss-up which of the two will win.)[6] You can think of allocating the total time you spend working each week to pursuing three types of goals:

- Rabbits: small, relatively easy to come by, with a low payoff after the goal is complete
- Antelopes: require more planning and effort, but relatively rewarding once you finish this work
- Giraffes: distant goals that require a lot of time, effort, and luck to achieve, but are a *big* victory if you are able to make them happen

Let's look at some examples. For an actor, a rabbit goal might be working as an extra in a movie or getting a part in an unpaid student film. These smaller goals keep us busy and give us a sense of progress, even though they don't make a big dent individually. An antelope goal might be getting a speaking role in a movie or having your content go viral. These midsize goals are ones that we hope to repeat regularly. A giraffe goal could be becoming a series regular in a television show, or as big as winning an Oscar. These large, long-term goals may happen once in a lifetime, or not at all. Still, they can keep us inspired and motivated over time.

You'll notice that in each case, one goal was work that will pay you today; the other was an accolade that might help you bring in more income down the line. If we are very passionate about the work we are doing, sometimes the accolades will be more seductive than the financial outcomes. Check that you have an even balance between financial and prestige goals. If you are saving money to accomplish a nonwork goal, like buying a home, estimate the amount of money you'll need and write that down too so that you can get specific on what your business plan needs to achieve.

Just as all of us need a mix of different food groups to have a nutritious diet, our careers need a mix of small, moderate, and ambitious goals to stay balanced. The risk here is aiming too high or too low. If you only go after incredibly big and improbable goals, there is the very real chance that you'll run out of funds long before you achieve any of them. On the flip side, if you don't pause and check whether you can go after something bigger, you may find yourself working a lot but having very little money or energy to show for it.

Your goals might include dollar amounts you'd like to earn, projects you'd like to complete, or clients you'd like to work for. Whichever you choose, make sure these are specific. Chelsea Lorraine, an engineer and singer, does best when she avoids amorphous goals.

"My goals used to be very vague," she said.[7] She would set goals like "I want to work as a full-time voice teacher," but without a deadline, she found that time was passing and she wasn't moving any closer to her ideal outcome.

Now she's learned that her goals need to be measurable and also have a clear time frame attached to them that is not too far in the future. Her latest goal? "In the next two months, I want to create a group class."

THE RIGHT BALANCE

As you reflect on your goals, you might find that you are able to write down some goals of each size. But what is the right balance?

Large goals are simple: We can have no more than a handful of them at any given time. As one freelancer advised, "Set goals that seem impossible to reach. Don't settle for mediocre goals."[8] Having an elusive goal can keep you inspired. Several freelancers I interviewed reached their big goals early in their careers. They knew they were lucky and felt grateful. But they also felt adrift. Working decades later with nothing to strive for seemed more disorienting than they had expected.

It's useful to take time to determine whether you are someone who is inspired by large goals or intimidated by them. If the big goals energize you, keep your focus on them as you work through the tedious but necessary subtasks. If the reverse is true, notice how each small step you take is bringing you closer to something you never dreamed you might be able to achieve.

For Kristen Powell, an assistant store manager at Starbucks and music teacher, goals work best when she sets a stretch goal and then breaks it down into many smaller subtasks. She dreams of putting on a music recital, which would be a bigger creative and logistical undertaking than she has done before. That is her midsize goal, which she has now broken down into its component subgoals.

"If I just take baby steps and start working on one piece, then go on to the next, and the next, eventually I will have a whole recital program," she told me.[9]

For Gabe Peyton, a comedic rapper with the stage name 40AF, the reverse is true. Gabe has dreamt since childhood of hosting *Saturday Night Live*.[10] This giant goal motivates every song Gabe writes and every music video Gabe eventually shares on social media. Producing music and the accompanying video includes a lot of high-effort tasks, like watching hours of footage to find the right shot, but they feel worthwhile because they are all being guided by this larger vision.

Once you know whether the big goals or the smaller ones give you more energy, you can shift your attention accordingly. With the rest of our time, we should aim for as many midsize goals as possible and try to keep the smaller tasks in check. Often we'll find we dream of doing bigger work or having more money, but will spend the day getting to "inbox zero" instead of working on a pitch for a new client.

STAYING DISCIPLINED

Tilting the ratio in favor of midsize, repeatable goals can sometimes be difficult, especially if you're just starting out or if the market is in a downturn. The best advice here is to keep trying for antelopes, even if all you can find are rabbits. (We will talk more about scarcity in chapter 6.) But over time, aim to keep increasing the percentage of medium-size goals in your portfolio and decreasing the percent of time you spend on smaller tasks that you don't find fulfilling—financially or otherwise.

How do you keep the rabbits from overrunning your life? Kayla Gray, a consultant to freelancers, praises the benefits of investing in good systems.[11] She suggests that freelancers start by figuring out what their "zone of genius" is. In other words, what are you good at that your antelope—and eventually giraffe—clients want you to do? Once you know what that is and can reliably get these kinds of clients, automate or outsource everything else. In this way, you focus on what brings you as much revenue as possible, and you free up your time for the things that matter to you.

A NATURAL EVOLUTION

We may also find that our goals shape-shift over time. As we grow in our careers, today's antelope goals become tomorrow's rabbits. This gradual progression is what Shruti, the wedding planner, deliberately does in *Band Baaja Baaraat*. She starts as an unpaid intern for one of the top wedding planners in Delhi. At first, getting this job is a big victory. But after some training, Shruti moves on to organizing neighborhood weddings, then larger weddings. Each time she levels up in her career, she chooses a bigger goal to focus on. Once she has enough experience under her belt, she starts to pitch wealthy families to organize their luxury weddings. This part of her business expands enough that she is able to stop doing the neighborhood weddings and focus only on the high-end ones.

On the flip side, we may find that our goals move in the opposite direction as our limits change. In the beginning of my dad's career, a stretch goal was getting a promotion at work. When he was first diagnosed with ALS, a challenging goal became driving to pick me up from school. And toward the end of his battle with the disease, it was speaking a few sentences out loud. Though these goals were wildly different, achieving each one was a triumph. We are all much more than our work, and yet there seems to be a core human need to strive toward lofty goals. Whatever the nature of your personal stretch goal, take good care to find one.

BUILDING YOUR BUSINESS PLAN

Once you have a good sense of the mix of projects that can sustain you, it's time to think about how to go from your current business to one that can give you the quality of life you want. In the next chapter we will discuss how to structure your costs. For now, let's focus on growing your income.

Calibrating Your Income

A mix of active and passive income streams can help us calibrate the amount of time we spend on work. "Active" means you need to be physically present or engaged to earn that money. Consulting work, for which you get paid by the hour or by the project, is an example of an active stream, since your clients will expect you to be available and create something new for them. "Passive" means that once you've unlocked that stream of income, it can grow on its own, whether you are physically working on it at any particular moment or not. Setting up certain passive sources of income might involve a lot of effort (like writing a book), but we'll consider it passive because that effort is taken only once, no matter how many copies of the book are sold.

Some types of income might be either active or passive, depending on how you do them. For example, teaching a course is active if you lecture and meet with students at a set time every week. But it could also be passive if you prerecord your lessons and then allow students to buy those videos so they can complete the course on their own schedule. We can think of these as "hybrid" sources of income.

Think of all your current and potential sources of income. Next, mark them down as active, passive, or hybrid. The list might look like this:

Table 5.1. Types of Income Streams

Active	*Passive*	*Hybrid*
Consulting	Investing	Courses
Speaking	Books	Airbnb
Coaching	Templates	
Day Job	Merchandise	

Do you now have a mix of active and passive income streams? If not, what other versions of your existing services can you add to create more passive opportunities? Also, you'll want to do a reality check to make sure things you've labeled "passive" are as passive as they seem. Productivity expert Tiago Forte suggests comparing the percentage of revenue you earn from each item in your portfolio with the percentage of the time you spend on it.[12] If you are trying to figure out which goals are antelopes, this breakdown can be a really helpful indication of where your efforts are paying off. You can then double down on your most lucrative and most time-efficient offerings.

As you're looking at your overall offerings and price list, make sure you're building in ways for things to go *better* than planned. What offerings might the market value more than you do? Or what products could be appealing to more people than you can currently think of?

So often with freelancing, we can become so focused on the fear and uncertainty that we forget that good outcomes are also possible. Matthew Huff, a writer and part-time freelancer, told me, "The ideal situation is if everybody wants [your services]. . . . But I was like, 'That won't happen to me. What will happen to me is I will have no money and I will be on the street trying to busk by singing a song.'"[13] In reality, Matthew found a part-time job and later a repeat freelance client that eventually hired him full-time. Now he freelances on the side with his company's permission. No busking involved.

Growth

Now that you have the components of your portfolio, it is time to focus on growth. Here, the concept of a flywheel is especially useful. A flywheel is literally a wheel attached to a rotating axle. What makes it special is that turning this wheel creates momentum, which can magnify force. In other words, the more you crank the wheel, the faster it pushes the equipment attached to it.[14] The flywheel is often used as a metaphor for a thriving business where growth in one channel feeds growth in another.[15] For example, expanding your social media following might cause you to book more speaking engagements, which then rewards you with more social media followers, and the cycle repeats. This creates its own sort of momentum, and when the flywheel works, it feels as though the business is growing itself.

How can you create your own flywheel as a freelancer? Earlier, I listed the different monetization strategies a freelancer might have and whether they are active or passive. Before any client can buy your products or services, they must first discover you. So to grow, you'll need to invest some time (and maybe money) into helping people find you—especially the people who are likely to want your services.

The key to effective discovery is to avoid turning it into an endless pit of rabbit tasks (not to be confused with task rabbits, but I digress). Ask yourself, how can spending your time in one area increase your sales in another? For example, if you write a book, you might be better able to sell your courses and schedule speaking engagements. But your speaking engagements will also drive sales of your book. And your social media presence could drive both. Ultimately, you want to get this engine to propel itself and generate its own momentum. What discovery elements do you have in your portfolio? Can you automate or outsource any of them, as Kayla Gray suggested earlier? Doing so can be well worth the investment and much less expensive than you think, especially since it frees up more time to do the work that's most rewarding to you.

Here are some examples of discovery channels you might consider:

- Social media platform of your choice (building an engaged following that values your contributions)
- Consulting platforms (completing your profile and getting good reviews for your work)
- Press (interviews, podcasts, social media mentions, etc.)
- Communities (speaking, teaching, conferences, freelancer affiliate organizations)

Continuous Adjustment

Finally, remember that your business plan is an iterative process. Pay attention to market signals: things clients mention needing, which projects get renewed or canceled, which parts of your portfolio are performing the best or worst. As you obtain new information and find new opportunities, adjust your portfolio accordingly. This should also involve giving yourself a raise as you gain more experience and deliver work that your clients value highly. Since existing clients can balk at unexpected price increases, start by applying your new price to your new clients. As you build up more clients at the new rate, you will be better positioned if you decide to gently communicate that rate to your existing clients with less fear of losing them.

Band Baaja Baaraat is an inspiring story of a woman building her business from the ground up. It holds many lessons for freelancers, including how to choose a market, set goals, and build a business plan. The difference between freelancing and wedding planning, though, is that as freelancers we frequently sell our time, whereas Shruti builds a company with multiple full-time employees. In the next chapter we'll explore the unique relationship freelancers have with their time and how this relationship affects our decisions on monetization.

SUMMARY

- Get clear on your reasons for freelancing before building your business plan. Are you optimizing for money, time, experience, or something else?
- Carefully calibrate your goals over time so that you shift your energy away from high-effort, low-reward activities to pursuing goals that can pay off in a bigger way.
- A solid freelancer business plan begins with optimizing both your incomes (to include active and passive sources of money).

6

DEALING WITH SCARCITY AND WINDFALLS

Growing up near Boston, my friends and I were Red Sox fans.[1] There was just one problem: The Red Sox were cursed. Back in the early 1900s, the Red Sox were one of baseball's winningest teams. They held the record for most World Series wins for the first fifteen years of the championship title's existence. Their fortunes changed unexpectedly in 1918 when the Sox traded Babe Ruth, "the Bambino," to the New York Yankees, starting one of the most storied rivalries in baseball history.[2] After Babe Ruth's new contract was inked, the Red Sox stopped winning the World Series, even though they came heartbreakingly close many, many times. This record, known as the Curse of the Bambino, lasted eighty-six years and was one of the longest dry spells in sports history.

An entire generation of fans was born, lived a full life, and died during this time without seeing the curse reversed. Sometimes this is what being a freelancer feels like. "It's been eighty-six years since I sold a project!" we cry out as we shake our collective fists at the sky, nervously eyeing our bank balance and convincing ourselves that crashing on a friend's couch indefinitely wouldn't be that bad. They would still love us if we cooked them dinner with the groceries they bought, right?

Welcome to scarcity—one of the biggest pitfalls on the perilous freelance trail. Let's look at what scarcity is, why it can be so problematic, and how to manage it.

COPING WITH SCARCITY

A scarcity mindset means seeing the world through the lens of what you lack. The limited quantity could apply to money, time, clients, relationships, or even the number of followers on social media. Sometimes our perception of scarcity is accurate: what we think we are lacking is truly absent or scarce. Sometimes we are so stuck in thinking about what we don't have that we fail to notice when we do have it. A scarcity mindset is problematic for at least two reasons.[3] First, it is a significant drain on our mental resources. Second, that extra mental load causes us to miss opportunities. Freelancers experience scarcity of all varieties, but especially challenging is the unpredictability of our income. Some months, we'll earn really well; other months, we may earn nothing at all. In those leaner months, we might pitch client after client and nothing sticks. How can we handle these lows?

A classic psychology study may hold some clues. More than fifty years ago, psychologists Martin Seligman and Steven Maier ran several experiments whose findings remain a cornerstone of introductory psychology seminars, though their methods would likely not be considered ethical today.[4] These studies involved giving electric shocks to groups of dogs in different circumstances. One group of dogs could end the shocks early by pressing their noses against a panel. A second group, which received the same type of electric shocks, had no ability to end them. The day after this experiment, the dogs from both groups were placed in a "shuttle box," which is a cage that has a hurdle in the middle. Almost all the dogs who were able to stop the shocks on the first day figured out how to cross the hurdle and hide from the shocks on the second day. Sadly, most dogs who were given no control over the shocks on the first day did not even try to avoid them on the second day. They lay down and waited for the shocks to end instead. Seligman and Maier called the behavior of the second group "learned helplessness," a condition where someone does not try to solve a problem because they believe they have no control over the outcome.

What can we take away from these studies? When the world is giving you electric shocks, keep trying to make the shocks stop. During the Curse of the Bambino, Red Sox fans tried countless ways of reversing it. During a ten-game losing streak in 1976, the Red Sox enlisted Laurie Cabot, who was then the Official Witch of Massachusetts, to change their luck.[5] The Sox won the next game after hiring her, but the World Series curse remained intact.[6] Twenty-five years later, Sox fan Paul Giorgio was reportedly advised by a Tibetan Buddhist holy man to summit Mount Everest, burn a Yankees cap, and place a Red Sox cap there instead. He followed the lama's advice, but the team continued to lose.[7]

Finally, in 2004, three important things happened. One, Manny Ramirez hit a foul ball into the stands and it knocked out the two front teeth of sixteen-year-old Lee Gavin. Gavin lived at Babe Ruth's old farm, and his favorite player was Ramirez.[8] That day, the Yankees also lost 22–0 to the Cleveland Indians, making it the Yankees' worst loss in history.[9] Interesting. Two, musician Jimmy Buffett performed a comedy curse-breaking ceremony with an actor playing Babe Ruth and another actor doing some hocus-pocus to destroy the curse.[10] Three, the Red Sox defeated the Yankees for the American League Championship pennant, winning four games in a row after losing the first three.[11] They are still the only Major League Baseball team to have come back from this big a deficit.[12] A week later, the Red Sox won the World Series.[13] The curse was ended.

Did the superstitions and hocus pocus have anything to do with it? Science would tell you no. Whether Boston's streak was caused by luck, randomness, or some other factor, even the longest losing streaks end eventually. In statistics, this tendency toward normal is called *regression to the mean.*[14] If one sample is unusual, the next one will probably be more normal. The really high numbers balance out the really low numbers so that if you look at a large-enough sample, the result will be average. That's all well and good for statisticians, but as a freelancer, you might not have the luxury of just waiting for eighty-six years until your luck turns. Here are some things you can do to manage the times when work is slow and you are slipping into a scarcity mindset.

Acknowledge That It Is Temporary

First, start by taking a deep breath. Your situation may feel discouraging now, but this moment isn't going to last forever. Like everything else, your working situation will also eventually change. How can you help yourself feel more relaxed in this uncertainty, which is part and parcel of a freelance life? If you've been burning the midnight oil for a while, a forced break can be a great opportunity to catch up on rest and self-care. It can be really difficult as a freelancer to take breaks or even plan a vacation, because you don't know when the next project will come in. So when the work slows down, do your best to rest, exercise, relax, and make time for loved ones and anyone or anything else you've been neglecting. If you knew that you'd be back to work in a week or a month, are there things you would like to have done with this time? Can you do any of them now? Taking a meaningful break will help get your energy up so that you can bring the best version of yourself to your next project.

Check Your Costs

It can be difficult when you see money flowing out of your account each month, with very little coming in. One thing that helps is examining your costs. When I'm freelancing full-time, I like to have as many of my costs be as flexible as possible. In accounting, these are called *variable costs*, because they can change from month to month. For example, the amount you spend on Uber is variable. Because you're not locked into any contract, you can go an entire month spending zero dollars in this category if you need to. The alternative is a *fixed cost*, which you pay every month or year, no matter how much you use it. A mortgage is an example of a fixed cost. A bank will expect you to pay your mortgage even if you are traveling and didn't use your house for an entire month, because the amount you'll pay is set in advance. Some costs will technically be variable because you're not locked into a contract for them, but they are still essential to you. Examples might include medication or school tuition. Consider those costs as fixed. How high are your costs each month? How many expenses are fixed and how many are variable?

Once you have categorized your costs as fixed or variable, the next step is to check whether you have any savings. If yes, calculate how many months this amount could last you if you continued spending as much as you did last month. This length of time is your runway. Now let's do some disaster planning. Take a look at how much of last month's spending was variable and could be cut out if needed. Subtract that variable amount from last month's total expenses. Now calculate how many months you could live on your savings if you kept only your fixed costs. Cutting out variable expenses should hopefully give you a little breathing room. With this information, you can step back and think about how long you can afford to search for the next project without panicking. Hopefully you have more time than you first thought; if not, it's time to cast a wider net in your search. You may want to check if you are eligible for unemployment benefits, supplemental security income, professional grants, student loan forgiveness, or resources from the Small Business Association or Small Business Services agency in your state.

A Few Hints about Taxes

One of the trickiest and largest costs of freelancing that nobody warned me about was filing taxes. What makes taxes so difficult as a freelancer is that you first need to figure out how to file. (Are you an individual? A sole proprietor? Do you qualify as an S corporation?) Then you tackle what to file. (How much did you earn? Which purchases from your past year were business expenses?) Finally, you need to make sure you have enough money on hand to cover a tax bill. When you have a full-time job, your employer withholds a certain amount of money from each of your paychecks to cover taxes. Unlike employers, clients don't do tax planning for freelancers, so we need to plan sufficient taxes for ourselves in case we have a larger tax bill at the end of the year than we had expected. As freelance financial writer John Kador advised, "The hardest piece about freelancing is putting enough income aside for taxes. Filing quarterly taxes ensures that I won't have to cough up a large sum when I file my tax return."[15]

Now, this is not tax advice, but here are a few things I've learned that can make tax season go more smoothly for you. First, it is really helpful to have separate bank accounts and even credit cards for personal and business funds. Second, software can help a *lot* with your expense tracking. Quickbooks, Wave, and Found are three examples of expense-tracking software that can be especially useful to freelancers. John Choi, who builds robots as a freelancer, recommended checking in on your expenses every two to three months.[16] This way you know if you are profitable, and if you can afford the purchases you are planning to make. Finally, if you can afford a tax professional (perhaps even by hiring another freelancer), it can be well worth the expense.

Hone Your Pitch

If you aren't getting any work, you'll also want to check whether there is anything you can change about your process to make yourself more marketable. There are two possibilities here: The market has changed, or your pitch isn't landing. If the market has changed, investigate what kind of work is now being offered on freelancing platforms, job sites, and social media; talk with your friends. Can you apply your existing skill set to solving these new problems? For example, several freelance writers told me they had careers creating annual reports for companies. But eventually that style of long, glossy annual report fell out of favor as businesses released shorter reports written by their internal staff. So these writers shifted to writing corporate marketing materials and white papers instead. If there has been a similar shift in your industry, you may want to consider updating your marketing to make it clear that you are qualified, enthusiastic, and available for this new type of work.

Whether you are creating a new offering or not, breaks can be a good time to improve your pitch. Ask someone you trust if you can practice together. Show them your portfolio, résumé, or website, and ask how you can improve it. During the pandemic, I had several difficult months without work. Thinking the problem was my not pitching enough, I tried to put myself out there even more. Eventually I hit a wall and wondered why nothing was working out. I showed people my materials and discovered that because I felt willing to accept any job, my pitches lacked specificity. As a result, people had no clear idea of what I offered or why they should hire me to solve the problems they had at hand. I spent about a month analyzing the work I had done and what I hoped to do in the future. I tried out different pitches and updated my website. I finally focused on being "a consultant and creative," with a focus on compliance for fintech companies. Once I gained clarity about what I offered and matched it to specific needs I saw in the market, I started getting work again.

Learn a New Skill

You know that feeling when you're really busy but you have an idea or are curious about something? You think to yourself, *Oh, if I had more time, I would definitely try that.* It's a good practice to keep a list of those ideas so that when your work slows down, you can come back and try them. Ernie Valverde, a freelance video editor, uses the lean times to work on new projects that interest him. He offered this advice to freelancers in the famine part of a feast-or-famine cycle: "Make sure that, even though it's famine and you're working hard to try to find the next thing, you still edit something out of an old video or shoot some photography. Try something you haven't done before. Use that time of famine to really hone more of your skills."[17] If there are new skills that others in your industry have but you haven't learned, now is your time to invest in training. This way, you will come back to work even stronger.

Shift Your Mindset

Putting yourself out there and going on pitch after pitch with nothing to show for it is a real drag and can create a vicious cycle if you're not careful. If you let it bog you down, people will see that you're feeling low when they meet you and might not be as excited to work with you. Their less-than-positive impression could mean you miss out on potential jobs that you were otherwise qualified to do. You need to protect your mindset and your energy during the lulls of your career. When that right opportunity does come along, you'll want to put your best, most confident foot forward and convince a potential client that you are exactly the right person for the job.

To keep your energy up, make time for activities you love—maybe even some you aren't monetizing (see chapter 5). Resist the temptation to withdraw from your community; instead, spend time meeting new people in your field and nurturing existing relationships with people who help you feel inspired. Now might not be the time to check in with the naysaying and "I told you so" friends who don't understand why you don't have what they consider a normal career. Take some time to work through the exercises in chapter 7 for separating your work from your sense of self-worth. And, most importantly, have faith in yourself. Something will turn up if you keep looking.

SURVIVING A WINDFALL

Just as it feels like the bad times will last forever, the same is true when things are going well. Unfortunately, there are pitfalls even in the feast side of the feast-or-famine cycle. Sometimes we assume money will come in at this rate forever, so we start to splurge. When the cycle turns again, we have little to fall back on. Or we might work at a frantic pace and not make time for our health or relationships. We might get burned out. We might level up to new professional challenges and find that we need new emotional tools to manage them. So how can we make the most of an upturn in our professional lives while also taking care of ourselves? Let's review some steps we can take to manage the times when our business is booming.

Acknowledge That the Windfall Is Temporary

Wait . . . what? Isn't this how things are supposed to be? Kind of. Even if you have the perfect freelance offering and your business is growing at a breakneck speed, eventually the tide will turn. Your rate of growth will slow or may even pause. You *will* eventually get a breather whether you want one or not. Think about what you want to get out of this period of your life, and do your best to achieve that while the stars are aligned in your favor.

Celebrate (Responsibly)

You've worked hard to get here. Clients are knocking down your door, your bank balance is growing, and you're working at a job that was once just a distant dream. Take a moment—or two—to really honor that. It can be so easy to just jump right into the next item on your to-do list because, let's face it, you're busy now. But these milestone moments are special. Don't miss them.

Save, Save, Save!

For me, the hardest part of an up cycle is remembering to be diligent about saving. Sometimes when I'm coming out of a lull, there are a lot of purchases I've delayed making. Now that money is flowing in again, I feel as if I can just buy everything I want, when that would actually be a bad idea. Maybe this is something you only learn through experience, but the key to taking advantage of a windfall is to be as diligent about managing your costs as you were in a lull. Sally Collings, a freelance writer, told her daughter before she left for college, "Get used to living as a student. And then, when you get a job, keep living like a student. You'll save bucketloads of money."[18] That ability to save when times are good will be so helpful when you need to handle a big expense (like taxes) or whenever your next slow period hits. Start by figuring out the salary you need or expect to make from work, and during good times, stick to that and save the rest.

Connor Swenson, cofounder of Forgewell, thinks about saving today in terms of gifting yourself more peace of mind in the future. "Every dinner I don't go out to, every party I pass up . . . that's freedom on the other side," he said.[19]

Adding up even small incremental amounts will mean less worry if you hit a month where no clients want to hire you, or you want to decline an unpalatable project to focus on work you find more fulfilling. Since freelance incomes are cyclical and can be quite difficult to predict, your future self will almost certainly thank you for your discipline today.

Set Your Boundaries

One of the biggest challenges of a windfall is managing the frantic pace. Cara Barone, a nervous system and business coach, spoke of her clients' typical reaction to a windfall: "When money's coming in, people are in a fight-or-flight, go-go-go state. Because the money might run out. So they don't stop working. They don't know how to rest or take time off."[20] The key, Cara advises, is to make sure we incorporate more time for play into our life. Work is hard to say no to, and play feels difficult to say yes to, because we often feel guilty that we are not doing something more visibly productive. But our investment in time to play is what allows us to be creative, relaxed, and more effective when we do work.

Some freelancers also choose to set financial boundaries. Writer Matthew Huff used to take every project when he was just starting out.

Eventually he found himself working around the clock and feeling that the pace was unsustainable. So he did some math and made some trade-offs. He told himself, "Okay, this is how much money I want. This is how many pieces I need to write in order to get that. And that then makes my budget work. Once I hit that number of pieces, I don't necessarily need to work."[21] Once he crosses that threshold, he might still take new projects if they were especially interesting or could boost his credentials and relationships in the industry. If not, he said, "Once I hit that number, then I can watch *Emily in Paris* in peace."

Bring Other Freelancers Along

When work is slow, we look for help from anyone who can connect us, hire us, or educate us to reach the next level in our careers. When things are going well, it's time to return the favor. Figure out what you can do to help freelancers who might be struggling. It's great if you can hire other freelancers for work you need done. But if you can't, there are also free ways to help. Maybe you recommend a freelancer to someone who is hiring. Or you could create content from your experience and share that knowledge on social media. Doing so might take only a little effort on your part but can make a world of difference to someone else.

FINDING THE MIDDLE PATH

What's a freelancer to do? Buffeted by the waves that cause their earnings to rise and fall, a freelancer needs to avoid being distracted by either the crest of the waves or the troughs but instead plan around them, knowing these ebbs and flows will almost certainly happen. To truly adopt a freelance mindset, you must become a contrarian. You must connect with abundance when money is tight and save hard when you actually feel prosperous. This is the middle way. While our bank account has very real implications for the actions we can take, it is also an arbitrary string of numbers that can change at any time. Our worth, our self-belief, and our mood must come from somewhere else.

What makes the freelance mindset so powerful? We are constantly practicing re-centering ourselves by persevering through the lows and not being distracted by the highs. Month after month, year after year. And as a freelancer, you must take care of yourself. What does self-care look like in a freelance context? You can do several things to make sure you stay physically and mentally healthy.

Be Gentle with Yourself

Finding the middle path is the work of a lifetime, so be gentle with yourself when you aren't able to do it overnight. We all sometimes feel like the highs and lows of our careers—and lives—will last forever. Then we are shocked when our circumstances change again. Remember that developing a freelance mindset is not a race, and freelancing is not a zero-sum game. When you see other freelancers succeed, remember that they are making the pie bigger for all of us. Only when we have a critical mass of freelancers will the other things we all need come around, like policies for sick leave or renting or health insurance. In the meantime, the following paragraphs show some small, but meaningful, steps we can take now to make our futures feel more secure.

Take Care of Your Health

I can't stress the importance of health insurance enough. Nobody plans to have an accident or get sick, but in a country like the United States, where I am writing this, illness can be catastrophic. When I was thirteen, my dad got ALS, a deadly neurological disease also known as Lou Gehrig's disease. He could no longer work. My mom, who then worked part-time at a department store, scrambled to find a full-time job with health insurance. Somehow, she got one. This was a miracle because, over the next nine years, my dad was hospitalized in the intensive care unit eleven times. Each of these stays would have cost $500,000 without insurance. In total, these lifesaving interventions would have cost more than $5 million if we'd had to pay out of pocket. Realistically, though, if we'd had to pay out of pocket, we would have lost him in the first year of his disease.

Eventually my dad's illness became so advanced that keeping him alive would have cost $70,000 *a day*—and would not be covered by insurance. To prevent financial ruin by delaying the inevitable, my dad declined further treatment. Even though we lost him in the end, I am grateful for the many times his life was extended. Not everyone is so lucky.

How can freelancers prevent a similar situation? Good-quality health insurance is difficult to get when self-employed. It is expensive, and the best plans, which will let you see out-of-network doctors, are usually reserved for people in full-time jobs. I hope that will change. Until then, here are some options. First, you may be able to buy health insurance directly from your state using the marketplace at healthcare .gov. Second, depending on which state you live in, you may also have access to health insurance from professional organizations like the Freelancers' Union or the National Association for the Self-Employed. There may also be trade associations for freelancers in your profession that help with health insurance, such as The Actors Fund. If your income is low, you may qualify for Medicaid. If none of these options work, you can also try alternatives like medical cost sharing or medical subscriptions that offer routine testing, preventative care, and access to a physician.[22] Some large companies do offer benefits like health insurance to part-time employees, which can fit nicely within a career portfolio.[23] And if you have a good, ongoing relationship with one of your clients, you might ask whether health insurance is a possibility for you as part of your rate negotiations. No matter your health insurance status, consider this a friendly reminder to make time to eat well, exercise, and rest.

PLAN FOR YOUR FUTURE

As a freelancer, you must become more financially savvy than people in traditional employment positions. You won't have an employer to set you up with a 401(k) that could help you take action today to have a more comfortable tomorrow. This complicates saving for the future because, as freelancers, we need not only the confidence that we can afford to save some amount of our earnings until retirement age but also the drive to do all the administrative work to set up the right retirement savings plan. Having faith in our future earnings is incredibly difficult, especially when our current earnings are small. I avoided saving for retirement for the first decade of my career because I didn't think I could afford it. This was a mistake. Diony Cespedes, the founder of Sole Strivers' Financial Fitness, advises freelancers: "Start investing now. Don't wait until you reach some future 'success' point. Because of compound interest, the pennies you invest today can be worth much more than the dollars you invest tomorrow."[24] There is plenty of research showing that a tiny amount invested earlier will often be better than a larger amount invested later.[25] Even if you can spare only a few dollars to invest today, your future self may very well thank you for doing so.

On the administrative front, we are in luck. There are several approaches that can help us get retirement benefits that are comparable to those of full-time employees. First, you could open a self-employed 401(k), which would function quite similarly to the one you would get a traditional job.[26] With a self-employed 401(k) you contribute money from your pretax earnings to a tax-deferred retirement plan. A key difference between a self-employed 401(k) and traditional 401(k) is that self-employed individuals may be able to contribute as both the employee *and* the employer (because, well, that is what being self-employed means). In some cases, self-employed individuals may find they can actually contribute more to their 401(k) than would otherwise be possible with a full-time job at the same income level. These self-employed 401(k) accounts can be opened with an online broker. Another way to plan for the future while being self-employed is to open something called a SEP IRA.[27] Your contributions to these accounts are generally tax-deductible and flexible, although there is a penalty for withdrawing the funds before retirement age, just like with a 401(k). Several services have made SEP IRAs easy for freelancers to open with just a few clicks, like Betterment and Wealthfront. Of course, only a tax professional will be able to advise you properly on 401(k) and SEP IRA requirements for your particular circumstances, but this paragraph is meant to be a starting point so you can ask informed questions.

KEEP YOUR SKILLS SHARP

This is where freelancers really shine! We are closer to the market than anyone else because we are constantly pitching to new clients and demonstrating the value of our contributions to existing clients, who are under no obligation to keep us on their books. We must perform, and we must provide skills that are wanted. When our pitches don't close, we know it is either a mismatch of needs, a failure to communicate effectively, or a gap in our skills. For this reason, freelancers are far more likely to invest in skills training and continuing education than are workers with full-time jobs. We are constantly expanding our portfolios and our minds. We are never done. The training doesn't have to be expensive like college or graduate school. People get hired because of projects they do for free—write-ups they post on social media, software they code over a weekend. You can volunteer to help organizations you find interesting. Keep growing your network. YouTube, Udemy, Khan Academy, and the local library are all your friends.

Freelancing work can be unpredictable, leading to cycles of feasts and famine. When you are in the feast portion of a cycle, it feels like you will never run out of clients. But slow periods—or famines—can also hit, and we fear they will last forever. Both the highs and the lows have their pitfalls, but there are concrete steps we can take to manage them, such as acknowledging they are temporary, remaining disciplined about our savings and expenses, honing our skills, reinforcing our boundaries, and staying connected to our communities. By staying centered amid these ups and downs, you cultivate a freelance mindset that is more resilient and forward-thinking—one of your greatest superpowers as a freelancer.

SUMMARY

- Building a life as a freelancer is fraught with uncertainty. Learning how to weather periods of both scarce and abundant workloads is essential to your survival. Remember to take care of yourself no matter how many—or how few—clients are knocking on your door.

- Times of scarcity may feel eternal, but they, like everything else, are only temporary. Take care of yourself by using slow periods to manage your costs, refine your pitch, and learn a new skill.
- When work is abundant, celebrate your success while acknowledging that it is also temporary. Keep saving, set boundaries so you take care of yourself, and look for ways to bring other freelancers along.

III

BECOMING A HERO

7

IDENTITY AND WHAT DO YOU DO?

The cult classic movie *Romy and Michele's High School Reunion* centers on two best friends on the eve of their ten-year high school reunion. Romy and Michele spend their time designing quirky outfits, feeling fierce, and having fun. Their happy bubble bursts when they complete a pre-reunion survey and realize they haven't hit any conventional social milestones since graduation. Neither of them has a career, a child, or even a date. Terrified of facing their classmates with nothing to brag about, the two need a cover story. They decide to pretend they invented Post-it notes. Since the actual inventor isn't famous, Romy and Michele know their fake success story will dazzle their classmates.

They seem to be getting away with it until a loudmouthed business school graduate named Heather interrupts. She reveals that the actual inventor of the Post-it notes is a man named Art Fry from the 3M Company—not Romy or Michele.[1] Christy, the class bully, gets on stage and announces Romy and Michele's lie to the whole class. Everybody laughs.

Three times in the movie, someone asks the main characters, "What do you do?" Each time, the question leads the main characters to a revelation about their lives. Their answers are a testament to how loaded the phrase can be—and how much of our identity feels wrapped up in the answer.

I had a similar experience at my Harvard Business School five-year reunion, when I had just left a start-up to become a freelancer again. On the first night of the reunion, an acquaintance asked me what I did. I tried three times to give a coherent answer. Each time, I was met with a blank stare. All around me, people were congratulating one another's accomplishments. It was as if they were speaking a private language I couldn't access. When my JD/MBA reunion approached soon afterward, I skipped it entirely because my inability to answer the question "What do you do?" was too uncomfortable.

It turned out I was not alone. Several of the freelancers I interviewed had similar difficulties with the question "What do you do?" Ramita Ravi, an accomplished professional dancer, start-up founder, and design consultant said, "I truly avoid it."[2] Instead, she likes it when her friends introduce her, because they can focus on what they find interesting and relevant to them. "My career is confusing to explain. This was a really hard thing for me when I left school. People were working in finance and consulting, [or other] super traditional careers. My schedule was completely different from everyone I knew." That was equally true for her in dance and in design consulting, because she had a unique combination of jobs with little if any overlap. While professional dancers often have side jobs, very few work as design consultants. Similarly, very few design consultants are pursuing careers as professional dancers. This makes it hard for both groups to relate to each other, leaving Ramita caught between two worlds. "It's really lonely," she said.

THE OBSESSION WITH CORPORATE IDENTITY

The origins of our collective obsession with what we do for a living are often traced back to the Protestant work ethic. In *The Protestant Ethic and the Spirit of Capitalism*, German sociologist Max Weber coined the term "Protestant ethic" and argued that it was the reason capitalism flourished in Europe and then in the United States.[3] This ethic prized diligence, thriftiness, and efficiency in one's work. Having these qualities was a sign that the person was predestined to go to heaven. As the theory goes, this work ethic took hold in Europe and was eventually brought by the Puritans to North America and then to the rest of the world.

Fast-forward several hundred years to today, and the matter of what we do for a living has taken on a life of its own. This is true in the United States, where hustle culture has dominated for years, as high-powered suits compete over who is more sleep-deprived. But this focus on people's professions is not a uniquely American (or Puritan) phenomenon. In India, an entire caste system developed to classify people according to their occupation.[4] In China, the notion of 996 dominated many companies, whose employees were expected to work from 9:00 a.m. to 9:00 p.m. six days a week.[5] Both the caste system and 996 are now illegal, yet their legacy still exists, albeit unofficially. When you have little respite from what you do, your occupation can easily become confused with who you are. Our obsession with knowing other people's titles is out of control.

When you are a freelancer, you have no automatic job title. It's up to you to create one. And the question implied in these social systems is a haunting one: Without a job title, do you even exist?

The existential angst this question creates could be one reason people fear freelancing. After all, becoming a freelancer means killing the part of yourself that sees nine-to-five jobs as your path forward to both safety and social status. You will say goodbye to society's understanding of where you fit. Welcome to the most challenging stage of your freelancing journey: the death of your old identity and your rebirth with a new one.

THE DEATH OF YOUR OLD SELF

Whether it's a high school reunion, a job interview, or just a first date, at some point you may start to feel that your nine-to-five identity isn't working for you anymore. It doesn't accurately match your current lived experience, and it may not match where you hope to be in the future. You are caught in the middle of two worlds, the old and the new, and you can't go neatly back to where you were before you lived this experience. You can't unsee what you've seen as a freelancer; you can't unthink the possibility of setting your own schedule and focusing only on the projects that matter to you. You cannot go back to the old way of thinking, and yet your new form hasn't taken shape yet.

The challenge—and power—of the freelance mindset is to separate our identity from how we earn the money to pay for food, shelter, and everything else. After all, we are so much broader than how we make money. Our souls are so much richer. If you don't believe me, think back to when you were in elementary school. On any given day, you could read, solve math problems, compete in a sport, paint a picture, play make-believe, and then get back up the next morning and do it again. With so many activities, you could not pick one of them as your central identity. That was still something you were developing. Now, as an adult, you can give yourself permission to revisit that state of opportunity.

GRIEVING YOUR LOST IDENTITY

To be reborn, we need to acknowledge the full extent of the change taking place. Even if you are moving toward the life of your dreams, you may still feel a profound sense of loss. That loss creates grief. For some, the loss will center on the loss of professional identity—the version of yourself that you and others used to see. Others may grieve the loss of financial security. Perhaps you were a key breadwinner in your family and now rely on your partner's support. A third form of loss may involve your social identity; you may no longer feel part of a community or team, or feel you are simply not understood by the strangers you meet. Finally, there is the loss associated with letting go of a dream that didn't work out.[6] All these losses are legitimate and need to be grieved before you can move forward.

If you read this and wondered whether you even have permission to grieve over something like a loss of identity, you are not alone. Psychologist Traci Bank Cohen finds that her clients often feel as though they don't deserve to mourn something such as a lost identity—even if they find it upsetting.[7] This is known as disenfranchised grief.[8] The outside world often fails to recognize these losses as legitimate, and that lack of understanding can be incredibly disorientating for the person experiencing them.[9] Cohen notes that a large part of her role as a therapist is validating the sorrow that can come with life not turning out the way her clients had visualized it.[10] Having been there myself, I can attest to how confusing it feels to grieve something you once considered trivial. If you feel as though you've lost something in your transition from nine-to-five to freelancing, your sense of loss is valid. It is legitimate to grieve this loss.

So how do we do that? The answer is relatively simple, but that doesn't make it easy. The first step is to recognize that when you are experiencing a loss of identity, you need to grieve. That means recognizing that your sadness, confusion, or disorientation about your identity is a symptom of something larger. Next comes acceptance. Accept that your life is in transition, that it looks different from what you thought it would be, and that your relationships have shifted as a result. Give yourself grace. When you accept these things, you can be present with your feelings. Finally, you'll want to acknowledge which parts of your identity are under your control and surrender those that aren't. This process takes effort, practice, and a good deal of patience. Be gentle with yourself.[11] This work will take time. If you take anything away from this chapter, let it be this: You are not alone. And as always, consider speaking with a professional if you find your grief interferes with your daily functioning.

REBIRTH

What comes after death of, and grief over, a lost identity? The birth of a new identity, one that fits your new existence as a freelancer. We can picture this change as a majestic phoenix rising from the ashes of your previous self. How does this new identity emerge? Like an actual birth, there is a period of gestation during which you accept that something new is forming, although it hasn't hatched and flying is still just a distant dream. The gestation period is the messy middle, the misunderstood space. And you may live here for a while. I did. That's the moment when you're lost for words when someone asks what you do, when you feel as if you have more identities than you can express in a sentence or on a social media bio.

But if you allow this messy stage to take shape, you'll eventually have a breakthrough. You'll notice patterns in which professional identities feel good to latch on to, which ones spark conversations you'd like to continue, and which ones help you get clients or nail your job interview.

Make no mistake: Rebirth is a difficult process. Some people get stuck here for a long time. I did for years. Some decide it's too difficult and go back to their old professional identity. But those who persist emerge on the other side triumphant, reborn as heroes of the new world.

WHAT YOU DO IS NOT WHO YOU ARE

Let me repeat that: What you do is not who you are. Our capitalist society spends a lot of time trying to convince us that we are our work, but we don't have to fall for it.

Ultimately, most people have to do the difficult work of separating who they are from what they do for a living. Psychiatrist David Burns finds many of his patients assume—often without realizing—that their professional achievements are a proxy for how valuable they are as human beings. This assumption is problematic on many levels: It is untrue, impossible to satisfy, and creates a ripe environment for both anxiety and depression.[12]

Failure to separate yourself from your work can lead to poor performance. Why? Linking your self-image to your job makes it difficult to separate unfavorable work outcomes from your sense of self-worth. Passed over for a promotion? Product launch a flop? If you think these external outcomes say something meaningful about who you are and what you are worth as a human being, you're in for a lot of unhappiness.[13] You may also be less likely to take risks that could lead to growth, and to request and receive better pay, titles, or jobs.[14] Instead, separating your self-worth from your job performance can be a powerful inoculation against the inevitable highs and lows of working life. This frame of mind can make you more curious when things didn't go well, more open to taking risks and receiving constructive feedback, and more resilient in the long run.

And guess what: Freelancers grapple with self-image every single day. We are on the front lines, where our identities are tested every time we pitch a new client, meet an acquaintance, or try to make a big purchase. To be successful as a freelancer—to persist, to refine our pitches, to live in that space of uncertainty when people don't necessarily understand us—we have no choice but to come to terms with the fact that we are something bigger than the absence of a job title. We are the same person when we freelance and when we have a more conventional job. We are also the same person whether we don't get paid for several months or we get paid the same amount every two weeks. This steadiness of self allows us to anchor our identities around something bigger and more purposeful. We are pushed to think beyond where we are today and to discover why we love the work we do and where we hope to be in the future.

SEPARATING THE TWO IDENTITIES

If conflating professional identities with self-worth is a mainstream trend, undoing that work is a major goal of the mental health profession. Psychiatrist David Burns suggests a technique for correcting this false belief that also centers on the scenario of a school reunion.[15] In this role-playing exercise, one person plays a person with a highly prestigious and lucrative job. In the *Romy and Michele* example, this person could be the bully, Christie. The other person in Burns's exercise has a job that is much less prestigious or lucrative. So when Michele, who was unemployed, imagines Christie as the top-rated weather woman in Tucson, Michele could have simply acknowledged that although Christie has more fame and money, these qualities don't make her a better or more valuable person than she, Michele, is. Of course that's not nearly as fun as lying about inventing the formula for Post-it notes, but it might have made Michele feel better in the long run.

WHO ARE YOU?

"Who are you?" is the million-dollar question. It's also one of the most exciting parts of your journey. Now that your old professional identity is dead, you get to build a new identity from the ground up. Your new identity can include professional, personal, and social elements. This way, you can bring your whole self to the table, a relatively new phenomenon. A time long ago, when we worked in offices, we could show up in our professional attire, work for a bunch of hours, and then go home and be our "real" selves. But that world has gone away. Now we work where we live and turn our lives into content that people we barely know can see. In this new model, it is becoming increasingly hard to compartmentalize the different sides of ourselves. And this new arrangement might actually be a good thing, because we don't have a "work" self and a "real" self in quite the same fragmented and confusing way as would otherwise be the case. Instead, we have one self, and we must figure out how to integrate it into the various situations we find ourselves in.

To create a new identity, psychiatrist Dawn Brown proposes a four-step process.[16] The first step is to separate your professional and personal identities, which you have already done. Next, figure out which aspects of yourself you want to advertise. This step can be part aspirational. If you are just uncovering a new dimension of yourself, identifying with this new role mentally prepares you to grow into it. This revamped identity is also part informational, as it allows people to see the real you. Next, once you have a new identity in mind, take it out for a test drive. Analyze it from different perspectives and see if it holds up to your expectations. If not, iterate until it does. Get used to thinking of yourself as a software engineer, a dancer, or whatever other new labels you choose. Challenge yourself to use these new identities, even if you are a beginner or less accomplished in a space than you would like. If the identity feels meaningful to you, it is valid. There will always be room to improve your skills, no matter which level you are at. Finally, announce your new identity to the world! Say it at that dinner party, put it on your website, or update your social media profile.

SO, WHAT DO YOU DO?

The question of what you do for a living is not going away anytime soon in our culture, but we can learn to answer it in a concise way that still feels authentic to our lived experience. More than other workers, freelancers need to have their elevator pitches down pat. Perhaps you already can distill your experience into a single title or phrase, but if that isn't working for you, another approach is to use duality: "I'm this and this." Duality is easy to grasp because it is a framework that underpins our entire world. We have light and dark, action and reaction, good and bad. Plus our information-overloaded brains love to slot people into either-or boxes. When an "and" comes along, it's surprising and therefore memorable. The intersection of two separate domains becomes a mystery to unpack. Combining your different identities to showcase just the right amount of your uniqueness is what psychologist Marilynn

Brewer refers to as "optimal distinctiveness," or the human desire to simultaneously stand out from the crowd and fit in with a group.[17]

The other pattern that works well is arranging things into groups of three. Why three? That's an easy number for the mind to grasp. It's basically duality and one exception. The pattern works so well that the entire strategy-consulting industry revolves around synthesizing vast amounts of information into groups of three for busy executives before making a final recommendation. Barbara Minto, whose work on logic and organization has been used extensively by the consulting firm McKinsey & Company, notes that when the mind receives four or more pieces of information, it naturally starts organizing them into smaller groups in order to retain them.[18]

Do this proactively for your listener. Synthesize your experience into one, two, or three categories. Such a pattern will save you a lot of awkwardness and confusion. But how can you effectively break down the information into punchy and accurate categories if you have a nontraditional career or multiple ones? To find out, I spoke with Sarabeth Berk, the psychologist and expert on hybrid identities we met in chapter 4.

The topic of nontraditional professional identities has personal significance to Sarabeth, after experiencing something she describes as a "professional identity crisis" during graduate school.[19] While applying for jobs during her doctorate, Sarabeth found that none of the available roles felt right because they were too narrow. "I felt like I could only show up as one side of me, but I wanted to use all of me. I was really tired of turning on and off different parts of myself," she said. Up until this point, Sarabeth was always trying to fit into a box. Now she wanted a career where all her different identities were embraced, but she didn't think that was possible. That's when she realized what was actually the problem.

"I thought I was burned out or lost or just struggling to define my passion and purpose. I didn't know I was having an identity crisis," she said.

This realization drove Sarabeth to become curious about what a job title actually means, and she began studying how we are more than our job titles. She investigated how we can create optimal job titles for ourselves if our experiences don't map neatly into preexisting categories. Sarabeth recommends doing a brain dump of all your current professional identities then paring that list down to the primary ones, which are usually the ones you use the most, have the greatest amount of expertise in, and find more energizing. Finally, if you are someone who "wears many hats" (like she did) and doesn't understand the relationships between those hats in your work, Sarabeth recommends investing the intersections and overlapping spaces between your different professional identities.

I put Sarabeth's recommendations into practice and found some themes that worked well for me. If you find yourself in a similar situation, here are a few introductions you can use. Play around with the following scenarios, and see what response best fits your life situation.

- *You are pursuing more than three activities at once.* Find two or three themes into which you can group your different activities. For example, "I'm a corporate and a creative." This statement lets you include whatever you're doing on the corporate side at the moment (e.g., consulting, law, working in tech) and what you're doing on the creative side (e.g., writing, acting, dancing, painting) if the conversation continues. But this initial listing of themes is less of a mouthful to start.
- *You have three or fewer "hustles."* State them specifically (e.g., "I'm a writer and a photographer").
- *You are just starting out or exploring a new area.* Describe how you got there and where you're thinking of growing (e.g., "I'm in HR by trade and have recently started exploring event planning"). This approach packs even more of a punch if you can say why your new area (or its intersection with your old field) inspires you.
- *You are interviewing for a job or pitching a client.* Start with the experiences most relevant to your client and explain how they will help you solve that person's most pressing problems. Once you've demonstrated your competence in the subject in question, you can work in the other aspects later if the conversation allows.
- *You're completely lost.* Just say you're a freelancer. When they ask what type of freelancer you are, say you're still refining your niche and then talk about your favorite or most recent projects. If you have a dream project you'd like to work on, consider sharing that too.

QUESTIONS YOU CAN ASK INSTEAD OF "WHAT DO YOU DO?"

Another thing you can do to improve the situation is move the conversation in a direction that you find more enjoyable. This might mean branching out beyond the classic "What do you do?" conversation starter and moving into deeper aspects of people's lives. These questions—and others—give people the freedom to respond with things they want to talk about, which may or may not be their primary source of income:

- How do you spend your time?
- What are you looking forward to?
- What are you passionate about?
- What brings you to this event?
- Where are you from?
- What's something good that happened to you today?

However you choose to introduce yourself, do so with confidence. It's an iterative process. You'll keep refining your area of freelancing and how you describe it. Eventually you *will* land on something that feels authentic and resonates with listeners. While you do that work on your end, the world is changing, and a whole range of new responses is becoming increasingly common. So if somebody does react with a puzzled face, remember that *you* know who you are, and that's what counts the most. After all, your answer may just be the inspiration that person needed to think about their own career in a fresh way.

At the end of *Romy and Michele's High School Reunion*, when everybody discovers that the two friends had lied about inventing Post-it notes, Michele has an epiphany. She tells her friend, "Until you told me that our lives weren't good enough, I thought everything since high school was a blast. I think we should go back out there as ourselves . . . and just have fun like we always do. The hell with everyone else." And you know what? It works. The two have the time of their lives tearing up the dance floor with Michelle's new date. And the fashion editor of *Vogue* compliments their unique sense of style, leading them to start a fancy boutique for their very own clothing line.

As I'm writing this chapter, I'm also on the brink of my ten-year business school reunion. While I don't expect mine to work out anything like Romy and Michele's did, let's just say I'll be taking the message of authenticity to heart. And I hope you will too.

SUMMARY

- Creating a new identity as a freelancer may mean letting go of the life and career you had imagined for yourself. This transition can be both confusing and painful. Giving yourself permission to fully grieve these losses frees you to be reborn with a new identity.
- Freelance careers feel uniquely personal, but both shedding an old identity and donning a new one become easier if you learn to separate what you do for work from who you are as a person.
- When you introduce yourself, make it easier for others to understand your work by articulating a single specialty or grouping your work into no more than three subspecialties.

8

GROWTH AND DEVELOPMENT

Wilma Glodean Rudolph was born in 1940 in what is now Clarksville, Tennessee. She was the twentieth of twenty-two children in her family. As a baby, Wilma survived pneumonia and scarlet fever. Then she contracted polio and was paralyzed at only five years old. Doctors told her she would never walk again.

But Wilma and her mother wouldn't give up that easily.[1] Instead, they rode the bus a hundred miles to and from Nashville every week, which was the nearest place in the Jim Crow South where doctors would treat Black people who had polio. Wilma's family also massaged her leg four times a day, believing she could get better.

Eventually, Wilma's fortunes started to change. After a year, she could hop on one leg. At eight years old, she could walk with a leg brace. And when she was eleven years old, Wilma's mother found her outside, playing basketball. A year later, Wilma didn't need a leg brace at all.

Once she regained the use of her leg, Wilma excelled at sports. By the time she was sixteen, she was the youngest member of the 1956 US Olympic team. This distinction, by the way, came only *five* years after she started being able to run again. Wilma followed this up by shattering world records at the 1960 Olympics. She won three gold medals that year, the first American woman to do so in a single Olympiad. Wilma broke down barriers of race, gender, and disability and became known as "the fastest woman in the world."[2]

Wilma's accomplishments are exceptional. They are also aligned with how we typically characterize growth in our careers. First you learn to stand, then walk, then run, overcoming adversity at each step. You try different sports to learn where and how you excel. Then you train like hell until you reach your personal best, which, for Wilma Rudolph, happened to be much better than anyone else in the world.

The corporate equivalent to Wilma Rudolph's accomplishments would be something like working your way up to becoming CEO of a trillion-dollar company or founding a start-up that eventually goes public. Such an accomplishment looks a *little* different from freelancing. As one freelancer joked, "You do wonder, 'Am I where I should be for my age? How am I doing?' Because it's great that you're not in the rat race anymore, but then there are no other rats."[3]

So, what's a freelancer to do? How can we measure growth when the road we travel isn't marked by traditional milestones?

WAYS WE GROW OUR CAREERS

There are as many ways to grow in our freelance careers as there are people. This flexibility makes freelancing incredibly alluring, but sometimes that freedom can feel disorienting. Over the years, experts have proposed countless models or "shapes" that a career might follow. Here are some of the more common patterns that freelancers can use to categorize their career growth: the ladder, the jungle gym, and the portfolio. A final category, the kaleidoscope, describes the transition between the three other shapes over time. Let's look at each in turn.

The Ladder

The traditional way of thinking about a career is the ladder analogy. It implies that a career is something linear and that the goal is to go up. The fact that you are trying to climb upward in a single direction makes this career shape the easiest to quantify. In a corporate world, growth looks like a more senior title and better pay. You can also show progress by winning awards and getting a better ranking, if that concept exists in your industry. For a freelancer with a more linear path, some of these markers of success still apply. You know you're improving when you get a higher rate and are brought on for bigger or more complex projects. You can also measure your progress by the prestige of your clients. For example, Nate Garrido, a freelance graphic designer and illustrator, hopes to one day design Broadway posters. Growth here could look like first getting hired to design posters for a play, then designing posters for plays at bigger theaters or with more renowned actors, and eventually designing posters for plays that are actually on Broadway.

The Jungle Gym

A jungle gym takes the ladder metaphor to the next level, literally.[4] On the playground, jungle gyms are built from a hodgepodge of materials. They can include ladders for climbing in different directions, bars and rings to hang and swing on, and slides. As a career shape, the jungle gym suggests that sometimes the best decision for you is to change directions. You can move diagonally or sideways. The possibilities are infinite. They're also playful, even though they might feel scary at times.

If you encounter a jungle gym career in the wild (sorry for the pun), you might hear some other names for it: career lattice, infinite set of pipes, a squiggly career.[5] Since you can only play in one part of a jungle gym at a time, this career shape applies best to people who pivot from one specialty to another or who toggle between a couple of clearly defined specialties. An example of a freelancer on a jungle gym career is an attorney I spoke with. This person spent years climbing the ladder as a full-time lawyer.[6] Eventually, she realized it was time for a change. She left her law-firm job and started freelancing as a lawyer by setting up a profile on a major platform. On the side, she learned to write code. When she had the skills and information she needed, she reached out and grabbed on to a new section of her career jungle gym by finding a full-time job as a software engineer. What separates the jungle gym career from other career shapes is that you may switch industries or functions (which is not contemplated by the career ladder), but you are singularly focused on growing in one industry or skill set at any given time. Within that subspecialty, there are traditional milestones to define growth by how you are progressing on each individual track of raises, projects, titles, or promotions.

Portfolio

While jungle gyms are defined by the transitions you make between different, sequential careers, a portfolio career makes space for you to have multiple professional offerings at the same time. The portfolio career is the only career approach whose shape itself grows over time. It is also the only one that accounts for a multi-career lifestyle. The concept is inspired by investment portfolios, which are made up of different assets like stocks, bonds, real estate, crypto, and cash. A career portfolio comprises different jobs and skills that exist simultaneously.

Natasha Mehra is one such freelancer. She is a pharmacist/photographer/classical dancer/actor. Each vocation is meaningful for her, and she pursues them all simultaneously.[7] She has alternated between working full-time and part-time as a pharmacist, and divides the remainder of her time between photography, dance training and performance, and acting classes and auditions. Each component can grow: getting more responsibility at work, having a photograph or dance accepted at a festival, or booking a bigger acting role. Your overall career portfolio grows in two ways. First, when you add a new skill to it; second, when one of your existing skills grows.

You may also find, as Natasha has, that skills developed in one vocation bring considerable value to others. For example, Natasha's training as an actor has greatly improved her presentation skills and public speaking for her work in the pharmaceutical industry.

The portfolio has been used as a career model since the 1980s, but it recently became one of the fastest-growing career approaches for workers in the United States and the United Kingdom.[8] This rise in portfolio career models coincides with the explosive growth of freelancing. Along with the rising popularity came an explosion of new names for people in this category. People pursuing simultaneous careers or interests and are sometimes called *slashies*, *multihyphenates*, *multipotentialites*, *polymaths*, *hybrids*, and *multi-careerists*.[9]

Since portfolio careers are often associated with creativity, there are many creative career metaphors based on a portfolio approach.[10] One of my favorites, from futurist April Rinne, is the flower. Portfolio careers resemble a flower because you unfurl a new petal every time you take on a new skill, role, or industry.[11] As each new skill blossoms, your career grows sturdier and more beautiful over time, like a single, unified flower.

Kaleidoscope: Different Shapes at Different Times

Not sure which career shape fits you, or think you may have had more than one over your lifetime? There is a final model, known as the *kaleidoscope career*, which describes the transition you may experience when you go from a career ladder to a jungle gym or a portfolio.[12] In the kaleidoscope career, the puzzle pieces of roles and relationships fit together in beautiful and unexpected new arrangements when your priorities shift or when an experience causes you to view your life in a new light.

For example, in her TED Talk, which has been viewed more than one million times, Laura Berman Fortgang describes trying to get work as an actor on Broadway during her twenties.[13] She believed that if she succeeded as an actor, she could inspire people to change their lives. A decade later, when she had not reached the level of acting success she wanted, Laura went through a kaleidoscope career phase and realized that she had misunderstood her dream. Instead of acting to inspire people, she could focus directly on the inspiration piece. She pivoted to become an author, speaker, and career coach to help people find ways to change their lives. Her acting training was directly relevant, as it helped her tell stories and understand the human condition, preparing her for this new stage of her career. Voilà! The pieces of the puzzle finally fell into place, and she now had a new career portfolio.

When you are in the kaleidoscope stage, you are trying to make sense of what is happening in your career. Why are you not reaching your goals? Why is the work you've chosen not providing the same level of meaning you thought it would? Once you figure out what, if anything, needs to change, you can confidently reach for the next bar on your career jungle gym or add a new category to your portfolio. If only your mindset needs to change, you can work on reframing your perspective. Either way, the kaleidoscope describes the stage where you are understanding your circumstances and coming to a decision about what to do next.

VIEWING OUR CAREERS THROUGH A WIDER LENS

Understanding the different shapes a career may take can help us broaden our view of our own experiences. Returning to Wilma Rudolph, the story gets even more interesting *after* she won at the Olympics. Why? In the wake of her victory, Wilma had become an international celebrity. When she returned to Tennessee, she refused to attend the celebratory parade and gala in her honor if they were racially segregated. Given her fame, the town agreed. The celebration became the town's first integrated event, and thousands of people joined the festivities.[14]

Whoosh! Wilma had conquered the career ladder in her industry, yes, but she didn't stop there. Instead, she started adding new categories to her career—creating a portfolio. She added the role of civil rights activist to her role as an athlete, made many media appearances, wrote a book, and consulted on a movie about her life.[15] These additional skills and activities became additions to her career portfolio and new avenues for growth.

That's not all. Wilma Rudolph retired from running shortly after the 1960 Olympics and went back to school to train for a new career entirely. Her goal? To learn how to teach and coach others. Teaching now became her primary career and could be seen as switching ladders using the jungle gym career metaphor.

By the following Olympics, she was married with two children and recovering from an appendectomy that prevented her from running.[16] Her priorities had presumably changed. Wilma is later quoted as saying, "I have always believed that the most important aspect of my life is working with young people . . . It's been my dream to start programs that, through athletics, foster education."[17] Maybe this was her goal throughout, or maybe, like in a kaleidoscope, the new aspects of her life fit together in a way she wouldn't have predicted. Either way, Wilma's story is one of growth across multiple dimensions in the face of tremendous odds, and it continues long after her record-shattering Olympic gold medals.

HOW DO YOU DEFINE SUCCESS?

Once you identify the shape your career has taken so far, you can actively choose its shape for the future. That new shape will lead to new ways of growing and succeeding. Our potential for growth is infinite, but our time and energy are not. It's worthwhile, now, to pause to think about how you define success.

Kayla Gray, the portfolio careerist we met in chapter 5, told me, "I'm someone that likes to accomplish a lot in her day. And [only freelancing] didn't fill me up in the same way that collaborating with people solving big problems does. I need both [freelancing and full-time work]. But a good friend of mine just loves walking her dog in the mornings, and for her, that's her idea of perfection. When you set out to freelance, I think having the end in mind is actually really important."[18]

Ultimately, asking the questions and being honest with yourself about the answers can go a long way. Kayla, whose freelance business includes advising freelancers, suggests asking yourself several questions about what you want. These include "Do I want to leave my job, or do I just want a couple of extra hours in my day? Do I want to spend my nights working? Do I want to automate my business so that I don't have to work?"[19] These questions inform the choices you make daily when you are faced with trade-offs.

Since freelancing careers can take many shapes beyond the classic ladder, I asked the freelancers I interviewed how they defined success in their careers. Certain themes kept coming up in my conversations. Most people defined success along multiple dimensions, like income and relationships, or income and well-being. Others said they didn't know how they defined success and were in a more exploratory or intuitive state of understanding what works for them. Some, having achieved many of the following dimensions of success, then turned their focus to having a meaningful impact on the world.

Financial

Financial measures of success might not surprise you because (1) housing and food are essential, and (2) money is easy to measure.

For these reasons, income was the baseline definition of success for most freelancers I interviewed. Let's hear from two such interviewees:

Freelance writer Shalene Gupta uses income as a yardstick of success. "Very crudely," she says, "I have my income, and every year I hope to keep topping it. That's worked so far, but it's easy to do when your income is small."[20]

For Inna Kuznetsova, a freelance dance and figure skating teacher, growth could be measured by her client list. "First it was finding clients. Then having enough clients. Then having a waiting list of clients."[21]

Relationships

Especially when it came to relationships—and not just the romantic type—people told me they needed to actively push back on external definitions of success. To make relationships a priority, they had to ignore what society told them they should be chasing. Consider these examples.

Vyjayanthi Vadrevu, a freelance anthropologist and actor, consciously shifted her perspective. "First it was like, 'Oh, what can I achieve?' and now I want more of a community. Yeah, you could achieve all these things, but if there's not as many people to celebrate with, what's going on?"[22]

Dan Pinnolis, a freelance designer and coach said: "I still fall into the trappings of what success should be: certain income, career status. I think that's normal. When I can come back to myself, yes, those things are important to some extent. What I've come to realize is what's most important in my life is the relationships I have with people. If I have good relationships with people, that is success."[23]

Agency

A major part of freelancing's appeal is the ability to have agency over your own time and work. Here, two freelancers describe agency as a measure of success in their careers and also their lives.

Freelance writer Manya Chylinski said: "Success to me is being able to stay freelance—being able to build the life that I want. Being able to shape my life has been the biggest marker of my success."[24]

John Kador, who is also a freelance writer, described how the ability to work flexibly allowed him to participate more fully in other parts of his life: "Having control over my time and energy, that's the best part of freelancing, I think. And . . . work[ing] from home, where I could be a big part of my kids' lives."[25]

Impact

For some freelancers, impact was both an effect and a measure of success. Sometimes the impact could be defined internally, but often it could be measured by accomplishing certain milestones in the industry—other than pay. These could be the antelope and giraffe goals described in chapter 5. Here are two freelancers' take on impact as a measure of success.

Sally Collings, a freelance writer, has found that growth in her career allows her to take on projects that have a bigger impact. "I feel very passionately about working with people who wouldn't necessarily be heard if they weren't working with me, and who speak for other people who don't get heard as much. Whatever my earnings goals would be, if I achieved them without doing something I consider meaningful, I don't think I would feel successful."[26]

For Shalene, growth looks like the ability to have her voice heard when it otherwise might not have: "Growth in my writing. My ability to publish pieces in different places. I think a vision of the ideal future is one where I get to write whatever I want. I have the ability to publish wherever I want. I don't know how possible that is. But I think that at the end of the day, that is my definition of success—that I can pay my rent and feed myself and have that ability."[27]

Well-Being

Overall well-being was a measure of success for several freelancers, even if it was more intuitive than metric-based. They used their sense of well-being as a measure of whether their lifestyle and career were working for them. Consider these two examples.

Dan told me: "I know the feeling of what I'm going for. I don't know the metrics. I don't think that's helpful for me. A good life is feeling comfortable and safe, a lot of laughter. I have a dog and a cat. They bring so much joy into my life. This is good. This feels successful."[28]

For Paul Millerd, a freelance content creator and writer, success means continuing to work on his own terms so he can bring good energy to those around him. He said, "I want to have the space to create, and spend meaningful time with the people I love and show up as someone who is optimistic and happy. My goal is just to live a life that feels energizing, exciting, and honest."[29]

How do you define success? Which dimensions are most important to you? How would you like them to evolve over time?

HOW DO YOU GROW?

Knowing your own definition of success is one thing, but how, exactly, do you get there? The beauty and opportunity of freelancing lies in the ability to chart your own path. That glorious freedom comes at the price of, well, actually *having* to chart your own path. Since you're not plopped into a structured job with a large cohort of peers, standardized feedback, and regular performance reviews along the way, the freelance mindset means cultivating the right inner and outer environments to succeed.

Internal Resources: Curiosity and Openness

The inner environment starts with (1) the desire to learn and (2) openness to situations that can help you grow. Freelancers are incredibly good learners. We have to be if we want to stay competitive and keep getting clients. And since many of us have a fierce independent streak, we are much more likely to be self-taught than non-freelancers are. A study by Upwork found that 59 percent of freelancers had participated in skills training in the previous six months, as compared with 36 percent of non-freelancers.[30] And an even higher percentage of freelancers participated in skills training than did non-freelancers.[31] Freelancers generally seek out—and pay for—this training themselves.

So how do we go about learning new skills? The freelance mindset begins with curiosity. For Max Fucci, a videographer, this starts with wanting to know what everyone around him knows. He told me: "I'm competitive by nature because I play sports. [My clients] might keep telling me about this other person because they know how to do something. So I like to learn everything about where I'm working."[32] This attitude might mean researching online, experimenting with different processes, or reading books like this one. Manya Chylinski, a freelancer and former research librarian, said that when she gets a project in a new industry, she follows a systematic approach: "[Say] I have to write a twenty-five-question survey on these kinds of topics. Okay, *boom*. Let me try to figure out what are the best practices for writing a survey. Start reading, start searching, start finding the sources that look credible."[33] With all that information at her fingertips, she created her very first survey and had a happy client.

This leads to the second part of having the right inner environment to grow: being open to situations that can help you grow. Freelancer after freelancer told me that when you're starting out, you should say yes to everything—even if you've never done it before.[34] Sometimes *especially* if you've never done it before. Why? That's how you grow skills and relationships as a freelancer. And through that growth, you also add something new to your portfolio—some new skill that somebody, somewhere, is willing to buy. Of course, saying yes to everything is more of a guiding light than a hard-and-fast rule. Those same freelancers told me they decline projects that would violate their ethics or whose clients seem questionable. One freelancer told me he turned down lucrative offers from the tobacco industry. Boundaries are essential. But the freelancers' lesson is this: Trust in your abilities to grow to meet a challenge. Don't let self-doubt ever be the reason to say no.

External Support: Mentors, Peers, and Role Models

Many of us, including me, can find it frightening to do a new type of project. How do we grow to overcome this fear? That's where getting our outer environment right makes all the difference.

Having a strong community can be incredibly helpful. Many freelancers told me the hardest part of freelancing was the isolation. So what did they do? They created community when they needed one. (To my fellow introvert friends, if solitude is what you love about freelancing, rock on. Let nobody force you to leave your hermit cave.) They organize lunches, join writing groups, attend conferences, post on forums, create messaging or even mastermind groups. The advantage of this type of networking, beyond filling the basic human need for connection, is that it also satisfies the basic freelance need for information. That information includes answers to a wide variety of questions, such as "How do I create a video effect that looks like an inkblot?" "How much do other freelancers with my qualifications earn?" "How can I negotiate my rate?"[35] These self-organized groups provide some of the information that might be missing without an office or a team setting. They also keep you going when the road of freelancing is too difficult.

Within the freelance community, there is also a specific need for mentors. Unlike employees in big companies, which can assign you a mentor or "buddy" to make sure you're figuring everything out okay, a freelancer might have difficulty finding someone to help fill that gap. Freelance writer John Kador mused: "I wish I had a more intentional mentor. Is it possible to ask for mentorship? Is that something we can do? Does it have to be offered? I don't know the answer."[36]

If people hesitate to ask for help, we can remember to proactively lift each other up. Videographer Ernie Valverde asks: "How can I help that person that's just starting off? It's always about the giving back. Because we're always receiving, right? Whether it's the big break, whether it's having that person who saw something in you. Now it's up to you to do the same for others."[37]

You might be thinking, "I would like to help someone, but I'm not that successful yet." We'll discuss impostor syndrome more in the next chapter, but Kayla reminds us, "You don't need to know everything. You just need to know incrementally more than the other person in order to provide value. Even if to you it seems obvious or insignificant, to another person it could be the missing [puzzle] piece."[38]

For most freelancers I spoke with, their mentors were equally likely to give them information or help them get work somewhere else. Sometimes answering a quick question or a passing introduction to a potential client can make all the difference for a growing freelancer.

Mentors can be an amazing resource in helping you get to the next step of growth. But what about when you want to make a bigger leap? For freelancers, this step poses unique challenges. Our careers are so personally defined that it can be incredibly hard to find a role model. But the lack of a direct role model becomes an opportunity for freelancers. Instead of following in someone's footsteps (which we can never truly do anyway, nine-to-five job or not), we use other people's paths as inspiration but chart our own pathways. Wilma Rudolph could not have pointed to another American woman who won three Olympic gold medals, because she was the first one to do it. Like Wilma, you are the first to have your specific career path.

So who are role models for people with freelance mindsets?

It turns out your role models depend on what shape your career takes. If you have something like a ladder—a single specialty—your role model is often someone further along in that specialty than you. The writer Sally Collings, who we met earlier, could be considered a freelancer with a ladder-shaped career. She can name several other writers she admires or considers as role models for their work. Since a jungle gym career lets you switch ladders, you would find different role models for your different ladders. But what if you're a freelancer with a portfolio career? For now, you'll most likely have a portfolio of role models. Ramita Ravi, the dancer, design consultant, and start-up founder we met earlier, said she has "a handful of people" she looks up to separately in dance, consulting, and entrepreneurship.[39]

The breadth of career role models we have available is also expanding as we all reevaluate our relationships to work and life, and become more comfortable taking on multiple professional identities. When Ramita first started out, she was the only South Asian ballet and jazz dancer she knew. Now the field is shifting as more people pursue multiple careers. This shift adds diversity across the board (including to the arts) and creates role models for the next generation of artists. "There's a whole bucket of people who I aspire to be like [now]," she said. Our own growth can serve as a catalyst for growth around us by giving others confidence and inspiration to push forward themselves.

REIMAGINING GROWTH

While we may know whose career footsteps we'd like to follow, we can't re-create their journey entirely. We will still walk our own path, with its unique twists and triumphs along the way. So what happens when growth doesn't look like what we predicted?

We all have to reimagine our professional lives from time to time. For me, this happened when I wasn't earning enough money from acting to support myself financially. At first I felt disappointed and lost after deciding to leave Bollywood after just a few small projects. But over time I came to realize that the gifts I had received from that experience, while perhaps more intangible, were nevertheless valuable. Having had a taste of life on my own terms outside the nine-to-five world, I had broken out of my comfort zone. I had studied Hindi and acting. And I had spent truly meaningful time with my family in India—family members I had barely known before moving there because I grew up on the other side of the world.

Sometimes this perspective change is something you can do on your own. But when you're really spinning your wheels to grow, if you can afford it, a coach could help you crack the code. Jim Gallant, an advertising and marketing freelancer, discovered through working with his coach that his pricing strategy needed improvement. Now he's targeting much bigger projects, building stronger client relationships, and leveling up his personal brand.[40] Making these concrete changes in his business model has helped him grow toward his financial goals. An outside perspective can help you find inefficiencies and missed opportunities.

No matter the expert, remember to trust your own experience. Freelance consultant Jordan Hayles first hired a business coach to help meet her goal of consistent six-figure revenue each year.[41] Jordan's coach noted her strengths and encouraged her to move into sales. "Because my decisions had not been taking me where I wanted to go, I trusted more in her voice than I did in my own," Jordan reflected. She took the advice and moved into sales, but ultimately it proved to be a detour. "I don't think that's what I was really seeking," she said.

Jordan later discovered that her financial growth was being blocked by a need for emotional growth. She explained: "I went from 'Oh, I need a business coach' to 'Oh no, I need to learn about who I am.'" Meeting people who could support her on that internal journey was critical to her success. Through their guidance and deeper introspection on her skill set, Jordan has personalized her career in a way that feels authentic. This personalization is reflected by her unique job titles, which include director of intellectual creativity, dance ambassador, and director of great conversations.

The beauty of the freelance mindset is that it challenges our definition of what a career can look like. Instead of a standard-issue ladder that only goes up, we can change directions and move diagonally, like kids on a jungle gym. We can also create portfolios of sub-careers that add up to our entire professional identity. These choices give us flexibility in how we can measure growth, and they allow us to use the metrics that matter the most to us. The independence in our careers also gives us the opportunity to take ownership of our growth, but we can't do it alone. Just as Wilma Rudolph could not have become a record-breaking Olympian without parents who took her to the doctor, siblings who massaged her legs every day, and a coach who believed in her, we can't reach our full potential without community, mentors, role models, and coaches. They teach us how to lift ourselves up so that we can pass on the favor to those just behind us.

SUMMARY

- Growing a freelance career can take different shapes: linear, upward progress like climbing a career ladder; switching ladders like a child on a jungle gym; or a portfolio of simultaneous careers that grows with new skills or larger projects in each domain.
- Grow your career by identifying which career shape fits your ideal career vision, then finding metrics for success in the domains that matter to you, like finances, relationships, agency, impact, and well-being.
- Support your growth by nurturing internal resources (like curiosity and openness) and finding external resources (like mentors, peers, and role models) along the way.

9

WHAT HAPPENS WHEN YOU SUCCEED?

On their popular podcast, *Art Juice*, painters Alice Sheridan and Louise Fletcher talk about the weekly ups and downs of their working lives. The pair have achieved an enviable level of success as professional artists. And yet their daily routines look quite different from the endless stretches of inspired painting we would expect. In one episode, Louise describes spending a week by first getting an idea for a painting then editing her book, working with a web developer, tackling invoices and receipts, onboarding a new staff member, and setting up her business email account. When she finally sits down to create the painting she had imagined, Louise notices she can't breathe. It mystifies her, until she realizes that she is simply stressed by the length of her to-do list. While she and Alice recognize that everybody could write a similarly overwhelming to-do list, the two observe that they are lucky if they spend half their working time actively painting. The rest of their time is well spent doing the administrative and marketing tasks—like building relationships with potential buyers and galleries—that make having a career as a professional artist possible.[1]

When you're just starting out as a freelancer, it's tempting to think that all your problems will be solved if you just had a few more clients and a more solid footing in your career. It turns out that having more business may solve many problems, but leveling up brings its own set of challenges. Learning how to respond to these difficulties (sometimes over and over again) is the final stage of mastery in your freelance hero's journey. Let's explore some of the major challenges that might arise when you start to succeed.

BURNOUT

The first thing that happens when your business starts to succeed is that you will suddenly have less time. A lot less time. That might be exciting at first, because people finally want what you have to offer, but over time that excitement can quickly turn into exhaustion—or worse.

Cara Barone, a nervous system and business coach introduced earlier in the book, experienced burnout when she moved to London. She had been a high performer at work and extremely active in fitness and athletics, but eventually she reached a point where this changed. "I had such fatigue," she said. "No energy. A lot—a *lot*—of health conditions." Her exhaustion affected her far beyond the physical level. "I really lost my own identity, because I [had] always associated my identity with work and working out. So I had to figure out, who was I? What did I enjoy?"[2] This experience of burnout and health challenges became a catalyst for Cara to make deeper changes in her life and to help others around her find healthier ways of achieving their goals. She took a twelve-month life coaching certification and learned how to shift her mindset. Cara now coaches high-performing entrepreneurs on how to manage and release the stress that can come from being constantly online.

Burnout is about more than just being tired. It involves a constellation of emotions, including, yes, exhaustion, but also depression, anger, cynicism, irritability, and doubt in your own abilities.[3] It's different from stress because burnout feels never-ending or out of your control. It can come from work, your relationships, and ongoing family responsibilities. Stress that is temporary, which you know will end once you reach a certain goal, is much more manageable.[4] To tackle burnout, we need different tools in our arsenal.

Before we explore these tools, let's explore what causes burnout in the first place. One study of chief medical officers at thirty-five hospitals discovered that 69 percent rated their stress levels as "severe," "very severe," or "worst possible."[5] Surprisingly, say study authors Kandi Wiens and Annie McKee, most of this stressed-out bunch was actually not burned out. They explain that burnout is more likely to happen when people feel as though they can't "keep their stress under control." Although we'll never be able to control everything that happens to us, we can do our best to respond in healthier ways. Here are some ways to cope when we feel as if we could be burning out.

Set Boundaries

The ability to set boundaries comes from first realizing what we are actually capable of doing. We sometimes try to be there for everyone else and have a hard time admitting to ourselves that we can't do everything we want to do. I struggle with this all the time. I'll want to take on another project or more responsibility at work if I'm asked, but doing that has very real trade-offs. It means that sometimes I can't take care of myself and my physical health starts to suffer, or I'm not as present in my relationships with friends and family as I'd like to be.

Be Kinder to Yourself

So much of our stress is caused not by the situation itself but by our response to it. But worrying about things you can't change is a recipe for burnout. The eighth-century Buddhist monk Shantideva has a famous saying about our attitude to difficulties. It can be paraphrased as: "If a problem can be solved, what reason is there to be upset? If there is no possible solution, what use is there in being sad?"[6] This is easier said than done, especially for people with perfectionist tendencies. In the study of the chief medical officers, those who could persevere without burning out were especially skilled in realizing when their stress was self-created—and then taking steps to manage it by reframing the situation more positively and taking deep breaths when they felt their anxiety levels climbing.[7]

Carve Out Time for Self-Care

Making time for yourself is a challenge when there are endless demands on your plate. But to continue showing up for yourself and others in a useful way, you must also take care of yourself. What does self-care look like for you? For most people, it starts with meeting their basic physical needs, like rest, exercise, and a healthy diet. These will help you get to your baseline. The other part of this care is to actively refill your well. Cara, the business coach, advises her clients to make more time for play and to get out of autopilot mode: "We just do the things we have to do, and we forget what fun is like. That's when we lose our spark and zest for life. . . . To prevent burnout and to reduce stress, play is one of the most important things you can do."[8]

Cara receives some pushback from her more corporate clients, who believe that play "isn't efficient or productive." I've also had this misconception in the past. How can making a painting nobody will see, or singing an off-key song in the shower, help with my work? But Cara tells her clients, "When we are able to get into a more relaxed state, that is when we are creative. That is when we can have really deep focus on projects." Since I've started experimenting with more play in my life, I notice that I'm better able to focus and to compartmentalize the different aspects of my life. This practice has allowed me to be more present in my work and in the rest of my life, letting me show up more fully for both.

LOSING WHAT YOU LOVE

If your career grows enough, you'll eventually reach a new level where you're no longer doing the same work that attracted you in the first place. The *Art Juice* painters Louise Fletcher and Alice Sheridan started their careers because of their innate love of painting and creating. And then they had the good fortune that not all artists receive: They found a market. Through a lot of effort and discipline, the two have now built strong followings of people who want their work. One of the biggest surprises of their growth as artists is how little time they now have available to spend on creating their art—and how they must fight for it regularly. The rest of their time is spent on responding to emails, updating their mailing lists, managing their online course portals, recording and editing podcasts, creating content and engaging on social media, and managing logistics for their art exhibits. And the list goes on.[9]

This diversion from what we love is, in some ways, the opposite of what we expect to happen when we first start out on the freelance road. We think, "Oh, when my freelance career picks up, I can stop moonlighting in retail and have more time for my passion." But sometimes the pendulum swings to the opposite extreme and your career picks up so much that you don't have time for the work you were initially hoping to do. This development is one step beyond the feast part of the feast-or-famine cycle we examined in chapter 6. It's a sustained period of feast that changes the nature of the work you need to deliver. Here are a few strategies for navigating this new level of your career.

Reframe Your Thinking

When your work is requiring you to perform at a new level, you might need to elevate your thinking to match. This is the difference between a freelance mindset and just being a freelancer. A freelancer is at the mercy of clients, taking whatever projects come in, whenever they come in. Freelancers are replaceable. With a freelance mindset, you think of yourself as an entrepreneur. This mindset shift commits you to growth and puts you at the center of your independent career. It effectively gives your work a stamp of credibility. Danielle Langton, an entrepreneur and business strategy consultant, says the shift toward thinking of yourself as a business owner "makes you show up in a different way. It makes you think about your work in a more serious manner."[10] This understanding of yourself as a business owner then translates to the relationships you have with clients and customers. By legitimizing your business as its own entity to nurture and grow, you can sell more influential—and often more lucrative—projects.

Adjust Your Systems

When you find yourself at this stage of success, first take a step back, and resist the temptation to dive into the individual tasks on your daily to-do list. Instead, step back and look for patterns of tasks that you need to do over and over at different intervals. For example, you might release podcast episodes twice a month, post on social media three times a week, and schedule meetings five times a day. Many of those tasks could be batched so that you create all the content in one sitting and then use software to automatically release the posts according to a schedule you set. Or you can hire another freelancer or a virtual assistant to do these tasks in real time, as needed. Consultant Kayla Gray says, "Oftentimes, people will invest in systems too late, when they're on their way to two hundred thousand or three hundred thousand or even a million dollars in revenue, and they're running themselves ragged."[11]

It doesn't have to be that way. Instead, Kayla advises freelancers to get very clear about the specific area of work where they thrive, and ruthlessly outsource or automate everything else. If time is our most valuable and scarce resource, then delegation and automation allow us to spend it where it matters.

Actively Choose

Maybe none of the preceding options sound appealing. Maybe you think about how you enjoy spending your time and decide you're not interested in scaling up. That preference is valid. After all, to paraphrase Annie Dillard, our lifetimes are made up of a string of moments we consider ordinary.[12] If you want to free up the extra time to walk your dog, do that. Capitalism might be loud, but it isn't always right.

IMPOSTOR SYNDROME

Impostor syndrome is the belief that you've reached the current peak of your career as a fluke. While it's good to be humble and admit the very real role luck plays in all our lives, impostor syndrome takes this feeling one step too far. First identified in 1978, impostor syndrome refers to a mistaken belief that our achievements were a complete accident and that we played no part in bringing them about.[13] In other words, someone with this syndrome is unaware that their own hard work and skill collided with their good luck; they attribute their success to luck and luck alone.

Impostor syndrome is incredibly common. Many celebrities have admitted to struggling with this flavor of self-doubt, including Lady Gaga, Tom Hanks, Maya Angelou, Sheryl Sandberg, and Michelle Obama, but almost all of us experience it to some degree during our lives.[14] Impostor syndrome affects people of all genders and races, although women and underrepresented minorities often have to battle their internal impostor syndrome in addition to the discriminatory messages they receive from external barriers and prejudices.[15] Left unchecked, impostor syndrome can become paralyzing. Cara, in her coaching work with high-performing women, says that "impostor syndrome is the number one thing" that holds her clients back.[16]

Impostor syndrome can show up differently for different people, but author and researcher Valerie Young has identified some common archetypes:

Perfectionists hold themselves to unreasonably high standards and think that even a tiny mistake is a total failure.

Natural geniuses succeeded effortlessly in the past and think that having to apply effort now means they are somehow failing.

Experts won't take an action, such as speaking in a meeting or applying for a job, unless they have all the information or meet all the criteria possible.

Rugged individualists think it would be a failure to ask for help.

Superheroes think that they have to do more than everyone around them does and have to do it better.[17]

Perhaps more than one of these archetypes apply to you. For me, speaking up in meetings or in class has always been my kryptonite. In my first year of business school, I held the record for the person who had been cold-called the most by teachers because I refused to raise my hand. That's the fear of the expert impostor. I was so intimidated by my classmates who were smarter and more experienced than I was. I thought I couldn't contribute if I didn't know the answer to the teacher's question as well as an infinite number of questions that could possibly follow it. It was only later that I realized this perspective wasn't *entirely* useful and started to work toward changing it.

We all bump up against this self-doubt sometimes. Kristan Sargeant, a leadership coach we met earlier and who works with some very accomplished clients, said: "It's not that the ones who get the fancy gigs know what they are doing. It's that they trust themselves to figure it out. They believe they will find themselves the resources they need."

Here's how you can overcome impostor syndrome when you notice it taking hold.

Notice and Name Your Feelings

The first step to defusing impostor syndrome is to recognize what it is and when it is happening in the first place. Sometimes we can get so wrapped up in our thoughts that we start to think they are reality instead of just thoughts. Once we see that these feelings of fear are caused by specific thoughts, we stand a chance of doing something about those thoughts.

Examine the Evidence

If you think something is beyond your current skill set, keep in mind that you might have overcome something similar in the past. Cara advises her clients to create credibility lists. This is a list of every accomplishment you previously thought you could never achieve.[18] Now when I hesitate to speak up in meetings, I remind myself of the times I was cold-called as a student and nevertheless gave a reasonable answer. You can refer to this list and keep building on it whenever fear of being an impostor strikes.

Reframe Failure

If you're bumping up against more challenges than you expected, it can be extremely helpful to think of them not as failures but as learning opportunities. When you think of difficulties as failures, you assume that your skills are fixed at a certain level for your entire life. And if you stumble, you pessimistically believe that you simply lack the skill to reach the next level. Carol Dweck's research on fixed and growth mindsets shows that thinking about your skills in a fixed way like this stops you from reaching your best performance. If, however, you believe that your skills are something you can improve, the research shows that improvement is likely to happen. Seeing challenges as evidence that you are growing instead of evidence that you are failing can make a dramatic difference in your ability to overcome them.[19]

Get Support

Impostor syndrome is so common that almost everyone you know has likely felt it at some point. Talking to friends and mentors about your fears can help you surface what you are feeling and find new ways of overcoming these feelings. In my case, I told a friend how nervous I was to interview for my current job. I was so lucky that she responded by telling me to nip my impostor syndrome in the bud. Until she connected those dots for me, I hadn't questioned my own self-doubt or considered the possibility that I might actually have the ability to do this work at an acceptable level and that my perception diverged from reality. Impostor syndrome runs deep. You may want to work with a therapist to help you unlearn these thoughts so that you can be stronger going forward. But if you're in a pinch, film producer and entrepreneur Erwin Felicilda swears by this trick: Imagine it's your second time doing the scary thing, instead of the first. That helps Erwin calm his nerves and troubleshoot problems on the fly.[20] I found it surprisingly reassuring when I tried; perhaps it can shift your perspective in the moment too.

SHIFTING RELATIONSHIPS

Achieving our goals can sometimes change the dynamics in our relationships. As much as society tells us we'll have more friends and be happier the more we achieve, success can sometimes strain relationships in unexpected ways. In chapter 6 we saw how the freelance mindset involves confronting—and overcoming—a scarcity mindset, or the belief that if one person wins, another person necessarily loses. But not everyone we interact with will understand the limitations of the scarcity mindset or believe that win-win situations are feasible.

Relationships can often change when one person receives a windfall. Celebrities have long bemoaned the way their own increased wealth is matched by increased demands from family and friends. But the same can be true of successes that bring in far fewer dollars. For example, when an immigrant sends some of their earnings to family in their home country, the recipients' newfound prosperity can sometimes subject them to envy, suspicion, and fraying relationships with their neighbors and peers.[21]

Other times, relationships change for reasons beyond strictly financial ones. Friends and family might miss you if you are constantly working and unable to spend time together in the same ways as before or bond over similar experiences. Several freelancers in acting and writing told me about the envy that can show up in friendships when one person snags an agent, an audition, or an assignment. These can sometimes be quite small successes in the grand scheme of things. Getting an audition is not the same as securing a role. And yet misunderstandings can run deep, depending on how other people perceive the achievement.

Freelancers I interviewed shared a range of tips that have worked for them. One tip was to be generous (but sincere) with praising others. Another was to never complain to someone less successful than you. Self-deprecating humor, exposing your flaws, and making fun of yourself were useful for many—but these run the risk of sounding like humble brags, which are worse than outright bragging.[22] It's best if you actually don't take yourself too seriously. Some opted to keep a low profile. Others decided to ignore the haters. Many said they found out who their true friends were. What worked best for people depended on the specific relationship that was affected.

Ultimately, the envy was a function of both parties involved. Some behaviors could make envy less likely, but in the end, we cannot control how other people feel. All we can manage is how we respond to hearing about other people's accomplishments. If the green-eyed monster strikes, we can use envy as an indicator of what we desire and fuel for self-improvement. But if you're on the receiving end of someone else's envy, the experience makes you that much more appreciative of relationships that are genuinely supportive.

CREATING NEW SOURCES OF MEANING

The final challenge of success, which not everyone gets the privilege of tackling, is the curious feeling of disorientation that comes after achieving your goals. I spoke about this sense of loss in chapter 5, describing the different types of goals we chase, some of which should always be out of our reach. But sometimes we reach them anyway.

Michael Phelps, with a staggering twenty-three gold medals, the most decorated Olympian of all time, famously spoke about his struggles with anxiety and depression after the Olympics.[23] But we don't have to be Michael Phelps to wonder what is next for us. From writers to dancers, freelancers I interviewed in their seventies and eighties reflected on reaching their goals a decade or two into their careers and then having several decades ahead to find new sources of inspiration.[24]

Several post-goal freelancers credited their resilience to continually staying open to learning new things and finding new sources of inspiration. Broadening your perspective can be especially difficult if you have been laser-focused on achieving a single goal. For example, elite athletes often struggle to their new role in society after competing at the Olympics.[25] Journalist J. R. Thorpe describes the many ways these former Olympians created new sources of meaning for themselves after hitting the peak of their athletic careers, which ranged widely from teaching others to pursuing entirely new careers like business, law, medicine, and fashion.[26] A theme for those who successfully readjust seems to be a commitment to exploring new possibilities. This form of continual learning is essential to growing—and thriving—at any stage of your career.

Finis Jhung, the eighty-five-year-old ballet master we met in chapter 3, told me, "I'm very, very curious about learning things. I haven't stopped studying."[27] Even after fifty years of teaching ballet, he still introduces new concepts to his classes every few weeks to help students better understand and perform the technique. This curiosity can help you understand what motivates you and help as you build new relationships, train the next generation, or pivot into a new industry entirely.

Success in freelancing brings with it a new set of challenges that aren't always apparent when you first set out on your journey. They include burnout, busyness, the impostor syndrome, changing relationships, and a sense of purposelessness. By staying mindful and honest about the challenges you are experiencing, you can seek support and empower others to overcome similar blocks. Whether you experience all these downsides of success or just a few, becoming aware and learning to manage them is the final stage of mastery in the freelance journey.

You have now reached the apex of the freelance hero's journey. You have accepted the call into an unknown world and defeated formidable obstacles along the way. In the next section, we'll enter the final stage, where the triumphant hero decides what to do next.

SUMMARY

- Setting boundaries, developing systems to automate or outsource work, and carving out time for self-care can help you prevent burnout when your workload increases.
- Examine the evidence for your success, increase your comfort with failure, and cultivate a strong support system to combat impostor syndrome as your career grows.
- Find new sources of meaning for your work by staying curious about fresh perspectives and untapped inspiration.

IV

THE FUTURE

10

WHEN IS IT TIME FOR A CHANGE?

Max Fucci was at a crossroads in his life when I met him. After years of working "permalance" as a videographer, he finally had a stable full-time job that he loved. Having the security of a job in New York City also made him more desirable to clients as a freelancer on the side. What's more, his manager and coworkers fully supported his freelance work. Soon after Max got married, his wife was offered her dream job in Denver. The pair decided to move and start a new chapter of their lives. Unfortunately, Max's work in video production could not be done remotely, whether full-time or freelance. He now needed to decide whether to hold out for full-time employment in his industry or start from scratch and build up a new portfolio of freelance work locally in Denver. Adding to the decision was the couple's hopes to have their first child soon. A new child would add a depth of importance to stable income and benefits but would present a new trade-off to long hours at the office.

No freelance journey would be complete without a fork in the road. At some point, many of us hit a barrier to our freelancing and have to decide whether to stay the course or return to the nine-to-five world. In this chapter we'll explore some frameworks for making this decision as well as case studies for how other freelancers have decided.

THE TURNING POINT

When you reach a crossroads in your freelance career, chances are you're dealing with change in one of three areas: your inner world, your immediate circle, or the external world. By identifying which world is leading the way, you'll better understand what question you are solving and what to look for in your next working arrangement.

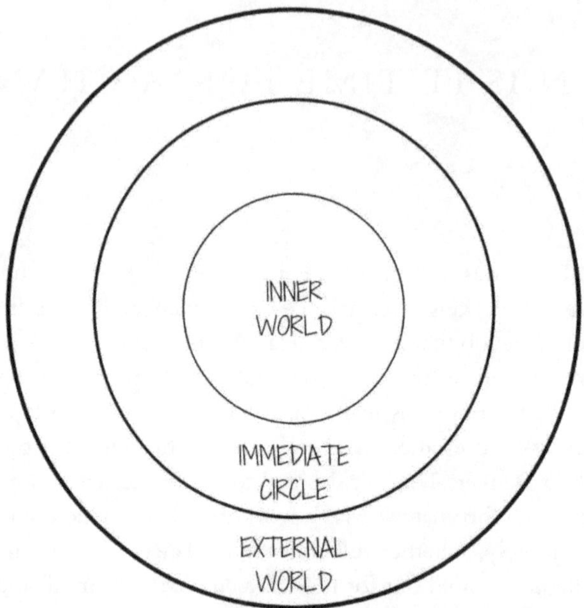

Figure 10.1. Three Areas Driving Change: Your Inner World, Your Immediate Circle, the External World. *Source*: Illustration by Tanaya Raj

Inner World

When your inner world leads you to consider a change, the decision is driven primarily by a decision to improve your own well-being. Maybe you're exhausted from having your existence be subject to the whims of your clients and the market, all while you manage every aspect of your business yourself. A stable nine-to-five job could sound more relaxing than constraining now. In some cases, you might have experienced a trauma, like one actor I know, whose heart broke when, after years of auditions, she was finally cast for her dream role and then the show was canceled before it even started. She has been working as a real estate agent ever since. Maybe monetizing your joy isn't worth it to you anymore. Maybe you are navigating a new health condition and need to change your work to be more sustainable. Or maybe you just want a more direct path to professional growth and feel as though you are stagnating solo. Several freelancers told me that working for a company was appealing because they could level up much faster and work on bigger projects.

When I made the transition from full-time freelance to part-time freelance with a day job, my reasons were a mix of the preceding ones, plus the desire to avoid the isolation that came from working alone in a pandemic. I really missed the feeling of being part of a team and working toward something much larger than myself. The freedom of freelancing can be alluring, but it also comes at a cost. Many workers who leave their jobs for independent careers eventually do return to more traditional full-time roles while continuing to freelance on the side for a taste of autonomy with less risk.[1]

Immediate Circle

Career transitions are often led by changes in your immediate circle. You could, like Max, be moving to support a loved one. You might be expecting your first child or becoming an empty nester. Perhaps you are dealing with new health issues and need insurance, sick time, or more flexibility. Maybe you are now a caregiver and need to be available to that person during daytime hours. In these cases, a job that previously worked for you suddenly no longer fits with the new relationship configurations and responsibilities you owe to your immediate circle. The new situation might be permanent or temporary, but for now, these changes in your environment fundamentally affect how you value different aspects of your working life.

External World

The third category of change is your external world. This change is driven by a development that is beyond your immediate circle, like the job market. Maybe there's a recession and full-time work is no longer available to you. Your industry of choice might be in decline or may have skyrocketed, radically altering the demand for your skill set. You might also be offered a job that is too good to pass up, like freelance engineer

John Choi, whose client invited him to work for their company full-time.[2] John had just graduated from an entrepreneurship program and was planning to grow his own business of building and selling robots. He realized, though, that a full-time job would help him learn important aspects of engineering that are difficult to explore as a freelancer, while also providing him with valuable income that would help him afford equipment and office space for his start-up. He accepted the job—with the caveat that he wanted to continue freelancing. Since his freelance work was what had put him on this employer's radar, they happily agreed.

By assessing your needs in each of these three areas—internal self, inner circle, and external world—you can prioritize what is most important to you in the next stage of your career and life. You can identify what your inner self needs, what responsibilities your outer self owes, and how the market's appetite for your work has evolved. Your new understanding can help you adjust the balance between full-time and freelance work (and any combination of those two). You might even want to revisit this chapter annually and check how the contents of each of these areas has shifted for you and how you hope they will evolve in the coming year.

What if, after considering the internal, immediate, and external aspects of your life, you are truly lost about what you want to do next? In that case, Dan Pinnolis, a freelance designer and coach, suggests getting out of analysis paralysis through a mood-board exercise borrowed from the design world. A mood board, Dan told me, is a design and branding exercise where you collect all the possible images and quotes that could represent a brand.[3] This is similar to a vision board, but the purpose of a mood board is to explore, whereas the purpose of a vision board is to inspire. Mood boards are often used for companies but can also be used to visualize your career.

Your mood board is meant to be eclectic, capturing a breadth of things that matter to you. It could include physical tools you use regularly, like a camera or a blender. It might include people or quotes that inspire you, including friends and mentors. You might add your favorite classes from school, your favorite books or TV shows, even your favorite vacation spots or activities. Just gather images of things you love without overthinking why. Once you've gathered this trove of visual and verbal inputs, you can examine it.

Dan encourages people to look for two things: common themes and idiosyncrasies. What connects the information you have gathered, and what is unusual or surprising that you wouldn't expect to be there? The common themes are usually where you devote the bulk of your energy, but when you're feeling stuck, it can be especially helpful to focus on the parts of your mood board that surprised you. Spend some time reflecting on what they mean for you and how you can incorporate more of them into your daily life.

WHAT COMES NEXT?

When the time comes to make a decision about what changes to make in your career, you may find you just want to change the kind of freelancing you do. In that case you can repeat the earlier steps in this book related to finding your niche. But it's also possible that your relationship to freelancing itself is changing—either because you want to do more of it, or less. Let's explore both of these scenarios now.

Doubling Down on Freelancing

Now that you've learned the ropes of freelancing, you may want to commit to it in an even bigger way. This shift may involve refining your business model to add new products and services while pruning your existing offerings to remove those that require the most energy for the least return. You may also want to do a similar exercise with your client list so you can focus on attracting the ideal type. Begin by listing the factors that matter to you in a client. Here are a few to consider as a starting point:

- How well they pay, especially as it relates to how time-consuming the work is
- How easy they are to work with
- How prestigious they are in your industry
- How much you are learning
- How much you enjoy the actual work

Try to identify the clients who score higher on these dimensions, as well as the clients that perhaps don't pay as well, don't value your work, offer little growth potential, or are generally high maintenance. Scaling up your freelancing should also involve improving the mix of clients you work with so that a higher percentage are within your sweet spot. When you get enough demand from your ideal clients, it may be time to let some of the less-favorable ones go.

To spare yourself a headache in the future, you may use these client-evaluating practices to develop policies in advance for deciding which clients you will accept. Policies, freelance writer John Kador told me, are effectively pre-made decisions. Every time the situation comes up again, you don't have to spend extra energy deciding how to respond. As an example, another freelance writer, who wished to remain anonymous, told me they would not create marketing content for a company that didn't have an in-house marketing department. Their rationale was that if the business doesn't value this function enough to invest in marketing in an ongoing way, this business was also unlikely to appreciate freelance marketing services. This lesson is one they learned the hard way, but it has served them well as a policy going forward.

Stepping Back from Freelancing

At some point, many freelancers eventually want to take a break from freelancing. The reason could stem from a change in any of their worlds. They might be tired or bored and thus feel an inner change. Or their immediate circle could be changing, such as with the addition of a new family member. Or they might see an external change: The job market might be hot, affording them a chance at a good position that was previously unavailable to them. You take your freelance mindset to your work, whether you have a traditional day job or not. This mindset means solving for your needs and putting yourself at the center of your career and life.

If you decide to scale back on your freelancing, you'll want to take three important steps. First, decide whether you'll keep any of your ongoing freelance projects. Second, let your clients know you are taking a new job in a way that doesn't burn bridges. Finally, collect testimonials and references to update your portfolio while everything is fresh. In the next chapter, we'll talk about how to market your skills as a freelancer so that you can land that full-time job.

WHO AND WHAT TO KEEP

Two questions arise when it comes to deciding which projects to keep: First, which projects are you *allowed* to keep? Second, which projects do you *want* to keep? For the first question, your new company's policies will matter, as will the kind of freelancing you plan to do. I spoke with many freelancers, especially in creative industries like writing and film, whose employers were very supportive of workers freelancing in their spare time. Videographer Ernie Valverde's employer supports freelancing because giving workers another creative outlet energizes them for their daily jobs.[4] Other employers encourage freelancing because it helps workers learn new skills, develop connections, and stay engaged with industry developments. Not every company will encourage its workers to freelance, but the world seems to be moving in this direction. Your employer's view of your taking on outside projects is important information to find out before you accept a job offer.

Even for companies with the most liberal freelance policies, there are a couple of restrictions. First, most employers would agree that your freelance work should not interfere with your full-time work. If you're MIA or spending entire workdays on your personal projects, your manager probably isn't going to love that. Second, your freelance work can't create a conflict of interest with your full-time work.

To better understand what conflicts of interest look like in a freelance context, I asked Erika Todd, a partner in employment law at Sullivan & Worcester, to explain. A conflict of interest, she told me, can appear if one person is active on two different sides of a transaction. Freelancers might find that their clients have goals that are in tension with each other. For example, if you work for a full-time design firm and also freelance as a designer on the side. If clients hire you as a freelancer instead of hiring your employer, that can be a problem.

In a minor case, Erika explained, conflicts of interest can cost you trust and business, but if the conflict is serious, there might be grounds for a lawsuit.[5] When it comes to managing conflicts of interest, honesty is always the best policy. Tell your employer early on and ask for their permission before you proceed, especially if your freelancing is in any way related to your day job. By getting their permission before you start work and being thoughtful about which freelancing projects you accept, you can avoid problems down the line.[6]

This raises the question of which clients, if any, you would want to keep. To answer this, you may want to review the earlier section, "Doubling Down on Freelancing," to find your ideal clients. I'd also caution you to be realistic about how much work you can actually take on during your free time. It can be tempting to want to do everything (trust me, this is my Achilles' heel), but that usually comes at a cost, like burnout or the inability to deliver. While it may be hard at first to say no to projects you enjoy, the situation is not unlike dating: Having scarce time can make you seem more desirable as a freelancer. For example, Max Fucci was pleasantly surprised to discover that having a day job changed how he interacted with freelance clients. "I can afford to say no right now. It's a leverage you didn't know you had."[7] His financial stability gave him more confidence asking for a higher rate or longer turnaround time.

AVOIDING BURNED BRIDGES

When you do decide to discontinue any of your existing projects, be compassionate and transparent about telling your client why you are moving on. It's usually best to give your client as much advance notice as possible—as the saying goes, bad news generally does get worse with time. Avoiding burned bridges can be a particularly delicate dance if the project was not one of your favorites. Perhaps the client was difficult to work with, or your final product did not match what they had imagined. For those cases, review the strategies we discussed in chapter 2. It is usually in your best interests to end all your client relationships on a good note, including the difficult ones. Even if you did not enjoy the experience, having a good relationship might give you leads to different projects if you ever decide to freelance again. If the client has ongoing work needs, consider referring them to other freelancers in your network who might be a better fit for their needs.

COLLECTING YOUR ACCOLADES

After coming this far in your freelance journey, you've probably done some great work along the way. It can be wise to memorialize some of the glowing reviews you've received so you can easily advertise your services if you decide to freelance again. If you do not already have a testimonials file, now is a great time to create one. Ideally you'll ask for a testimonial just after finishing a project for a happy client. It's always best to strike while the iron is hot, since that is when the client is at their most satisfied, and their memory of your contributions is freshest. First check whether the client has already written nice things about your work in a message, and save that compliment in your accolades folder. When the project is done, ask the client if you can add those compliments to your website or portfolio. If you don't have a message from that client you'd like to publicize, ask them directly if they would be willing to write a testimonial for your website, endorse you on LinkedIn, or rate you on a freelancing platform. If the project ended a while ago, you can still reach out and ask for a testimonial, but it may help to send a few bullet points explaining why you need the review and reminding them of your accomplishments during the engagement. These testimonials will not only help you win future clients but can also be handy to reread the next time impostor syndrome strikes.

RETURNING TO A NINE-TO-FIVE

Making the transition from freelance to traditional employment can be awkward at times. Transitioning in the opposite direction, from corporate to freelance, is often not a choice. It can be something you just fall into or get pushed into if you lose your job. But when you go from freelance to the workaday world, you're usually driven by something that appeals to you in the new job. Even when you have the best intentions, two areas can trip you up when you shift to corporate employment: not being in charge of your time and juggling professional identities.

Freelancers I interviewed have consistently said that the hardest part of moving from freelance to full-time employment was the lack of autonomy over their schedule. "I missed the flexibility of being a freelance writer," Matthew Huff told me, "because you can tailor your work hours to whatever is going on in your schedule."[8] The kind of flexibility Matt was referring to would mean being able to run in the afternoon or meet a friend for a long lunch and then finish work in the evening. "[My company] is pretty lenient anyways," he said, "but I can't just be like, 'Okay, I decided today I'm taking the afternoon off to go to the beach.' They're like, 'No. Let's not do that.'" Freelance marketer Jim Gallant told me he appreciated little things like being able to go for an afternoon walk or even doing a load of laundry during the day. Employers do best on this front when they foster a culture of asynchronous work, where people respond to messages instead of having to convene in meetings at the same time. Freelancers accepting jobs should be prepared to make this trade-off on their time but should have early conversations with their managers about the response time and availability expected from them and what they can reasonably deliver.

People who freelance in a field unrelated to their day job may struggle to manage multiple professional identities. There is a movement now to "bring your whole self to work," but that is not always realistic or useful—especially if your whole self is part of an underrepresented or potentially marginalized group.[9] To better understand this quandary of having multiple professional identities, including those that could be marginalized, I spoke with Kareem Khubchandani. Kareem's very own curriculum vitae epitomizes being a multi-identity professional with titles ranging from author and scholar to artist and drag performer.[10] In Kareem's experience, some kinds of work, like drag, are not always viewed by others as legitimate. A solution has been building a career that is focused on the performing arts and related fields, where Kareem's different professional identities support, rather than conflict, with one another.

If you find yourself in a situation where you have aspects of your identity that might not be relevant or even accepted by your new employer, consider how likely the employer is to find out about your other work. If it's publicly available or can be easily discovered, for example through a Google search or on social media, you may wish to proactively address it during your interview process. Briefly mention your side hustle, and follow with an explanation of how it makes you better at the role you are trying to get. Perhaps working in another trade makes you more creative or analytical, a better communicator and negotiator, or gives you some other transferable skill that you can apply to your new job.

The balance seems to lie in being transparent about your freelance work to the extent that the disclosure is relevant. The rest of the time when you are at work, focus on finding common ground, helping your company meet its goals, and otherwise doing the work you are being paid to do. Work is hard enough; there is no need to add an existential crisis on top of it by worrying that there is something wrong with either you or the company because the job doesn't feel like a spiritual calling. Separating your work from your sense of self, as we explored in chapter 7, makes you more resilient.[11] Just as you did for freelancing, you'll want to remember why you are working. Maybe having a job will help you level up in your freelance career by affording you better tools, classes, and support. Or maybe it will help with one of the three previously discussed worlds by providing you with health care or helping you afford a better place to live.

MASTER OF TWO WORLDS

Now that you have learned to navigate both the world of freelancing and the corporate world, like any hero you get to decide which world to stay in. Perhaps you'll stay a freelancer forever. But many people do eventually return to the corporate world in some capacity. The beauty of the freelance mindset is that full-time corporate and freelance are no longer mutually exclusive. When it's time for a change, your inner world, immediate circle, or external world will shift, and you can decide whether to dial your freelancing up or down. In the next chapter we'll explore how freelancers return to the corporate world transformed by their freelancing experience and new mindsets.

SUMMARY

- If it is time for a change in your freelance business, consider your inner world, immediate circle, and external world when deciding whether to double down or scale back.

- To double down on your ideal client, consider factors like compensation, relationship quality, prestige, intellectual stimulation, and how much you enjoy the work so you can target similar projects.
- End your projects graciously with as much lead time as possible, and collect testimonials from happy clients if you decide to step back from freelancing.

11

YOUR FREELANCE JOURNEY TRANSFORMS YOU

Kayla Gray was happily self-employed and building her consulting business of several years when a headhunter contacted her out of the blue.[1] The recruiter had seen Kayla's presence on social media and was intrigued by the savvy advice she shared with her following of small-business owners. Kayla received a plum job offer in the construction industry, where she swapped her blazers for a hard hat and steel-toed boots. She was excited by the prospect of working on a team, a tantalizing path to growth, and the chance to use a different part of her brain. The best part was that, since she had been recruited for her success at freelance work, the company supported her decision to continue freelancing in her spare time. Kayla now spends her days as an executive in the construction industry and her nights and weekends as a strategy consultant advising female founders.

"I need both," she said, referring to the freedom of freelancing and the collegial nature of a corporate job. "When I went from a corporate job to full-time side hustling, I realized that entrepreneurship wasn't what I wanted to do full time. . . . It didn't fill me up in the same way as collaborating with people and solving big problems did."[2] Having held a full-time job before becoming a full-time freelancer, Kayla discovered the optimal blend for her now was working full-time and freelance simultaneously—although that was not the case at other points in her professional journey.

If you have experienced both the freelance and the traditional employment worlds, you have earned the luxury of choosing which world you prefer. You are now also uniquely positioned to articulate what value you as a freelancer bring to any work situation and to advocate for other freelancers who may not yet have seats at the table. Whether you return to the workaday world or double down on freelancing, the journey has transformed you.

REBRANDING THE FREELANCE SKILL SET

As a freelancer interviewing for a full-time job or pitching a new client, you'll need to justify what you bring to the table. The context matters here, so depending on whom you are talking to and what kind of role it is, this conversation might be challenging. For one thing, many hiring managers still lack the experience of being freelancers themselves. They don't know how to value the distinctive skill set that running a freelance business confers. I once interviewed for a job at a massive tech company where one manager stared at my résumé for an uncomfortably long time. "But, why haven't you *done* anything yet?" he asked, gesturing at my thirteen years of professional experience. This was not a question I had even thought to practice answering. So I am writing this section in the hopes that, first, you are never asked this question, but, if you are, that you can have a killer answer.

One of the strange paradoxes of the working world is that entrepreneurship is fetishized and freelancing is stigmatized.[3] There is the misperception that freelancers are not serious about their work. Consciously or not, many people mistakenly believe freelancers are mere hobbyists who cannot hold down a job, are bad at working with people, or lack ambition. An article on the freelancing platform Fiverr advises people to avoid using the word "freelancer" outside their own freelance bubble: "People hear 'freelance' and too often assume underemployed, directionless, and unprofessional."[4] A quick online search turned up essay after essay about why freelancers stopped calling themselves freelancers.[5] We clearly have a branding problem.

Let's compare these common descriptions of freelancers with the list of qualities people associate with entrepreneurs. The business world is filled with advice on how and why to hire "entrepreneurial leaders."[6] One article in *Harvard Business Review* says that entrepreneurs are "more comfortable with risk," "driven by a need to own products, projects, and initiatives," and "curious seekers of adventure, learning, and opportunity."[7] Hang on! Does this description sound familiar? If entrepreneurs are people with all these traits, then freelancers are surely entrepreneurs!

Several freelancers I interviewed expressed their frustration that people don't understand how entrepreneurial you have to be to start freelancing and to continue doing it over time.[8] "You have to be so extraordinary to be able to juggle this many different things," Ramita Ravi lamented.[9] Freelancers, she said, "are so smart and resilient and dynamic. They're able to approach problems in such a unique way. There are so many unspoken skills that you build that I wish people knew."

We've explored many of these skills in the book: building comfort with uncertainty, developing a business plan, crafting new identities, becoming resilient to professional highs and lows, and other skills. These capabilities are on top of the many skills freelancers must have just to stay in business: sales, pricing, strategy, branding, marketing, finance, contracts, negotiation, client relationship management, leadership, team management, and so on. Never mind that freelancers are a highly autonomous, self-motivated, curious, gritty, and independent bunch with a we'll-figure-it-out attitude. These descriptions apply especially to freelancers of today, many of whom have embarked on their career journeys without a well-worn trail to follow.[10] There is no clear, single view of what a freelance career and life can even look like. "Everyone thinks being an entrepreneur more traditionally builds those skills," says Ramita. "Freelancers have been doing the same things, [but] no one gives them credit for it. . . . I actually felt more prepared and secure to be an entrepreneur because I was already essentially doing it as a freelancer!"

One solution to the business world's less-than-favorable view of freelancing is to stop using the word "freelancer" entirely, as the previously mentioned articles suggested. This tactic, of course, does nothing to help reduce the stigma associated with the word, but it can help individual freelancers get where they want to go. Self-employed workers who reject the "freelancer" label will sometimes lean in to the prestige associated with being an entrepreneur and use that title for themselves instead. The "entrepreneur" label can be a perfect fit when you are scaling your business. But if you've reached a steady state that you're satisfied with, many hiring managers will ask why you chose not to grow your business further. Their question suggests that if you're satisfied with your own business, you wouldn't help them grow theirs.

Other freelancers avoid the label issue entirely by dropping the word "freelance" and just describing their trade: writer, dancer, engineer, therapist, and so on. The use of specific descriptors can be quite effective because it shifts the focus to your particular accomplishments in that field. You might also consider using the comparable job title in your industry—like product manager—and then adding the word "fractional," "virtual," or "contract" in front of it. Some people create their own job titles entirely, like "Creative Disruptor" or "Director of Intellectual Creativity."[11] This group pushes the idea of a job title in a way that pinpoints the person's individual superpowers, reveals their personality, and intrigues the listener.

The approach that's best for you will depend as much on you as it does on your audience. How you describe yourself should (1) feel good to you, (2) be understandable to your listener, and (3) highlight your unique aspects that you want to share. The freelance mindset will stay with you, no matter what your title is.

Since there is a gap in experience between freelancers looking for work and the managers with the power to hire us, we collectively need to educate others on the diverse skills we bring, simply because of our freelance experience. Before your next pitch or interview, I suggest taking some time to reflect on your accomplishments in your specific field—as you would, anyway—by refreshing your résumé or portfolio. Then you could reflect on the skills that being a freelancer in that field has taught you—skills you might not have learned if you had taken a different path. These skills will depend on your experience but might include things like managing a business, selling to clients and managing that relationship, being a self-starter, having more breadth or depth of experience, or being more creative and resilient.

WHEN MANAGERS HIRE FREELANCERS: AN ENTERTAINMENT INDUSTRY EXAMPLE

The next step toward closing the gap between managers' and freelancers' understanding of each other is to explore the manager's perspective of why they may choose to hire a freelancer. Investigating managers' motivations will help you make a more effective pitch to sell your freelance services to a potential client. This perspective may also serve you well if you win a big freelance project or find yourself in a full-time job where you can consider hiring other freelancers.

Assuming there is more work than one person can do alone, when is it time to hire a freelancer, and when is it better to have somebody on staff? Depending on the scope of work available, the answers will fall on a spectrum. At one end of the spectrum, a project is eminently suitable for freelance work. At the other end, projects are more suitable for traditional employees. And in between, a project's need for freelancers is more varied. Let's turn to the film and television industry for a simplified example.

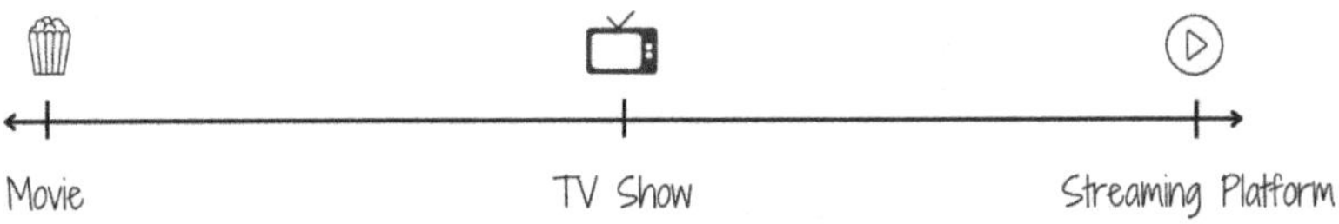

Figure 11.1. Spectrum of Project Types from Most to Least Freelance-Friendly. *Source*: Illustration by Tanaya Raj

Movies

At the most freelance-friendly end of the spectrum is the movie production model. When a film is made, an entire collection of freelancers comes together for the sole purpose of bringing the movie to life. This team includes actors, a director, camera operators, sound technicians, hair and makeup artists, costume designers, and many, many more workers. Each of these people is a freelancer. They have been vetted and selected for one specific role. After the movie is made, these freelancers disband and go their separate ways. Even if they are not making a movie, managers might have a project they know is a onetime thing. It may need more people or more skill sets than one person can reasonably provide. This is the ideal time to hire freelancers if the manager can afford it. Hiring full-time employees would probably not make sense because when this project ends, it will probably be a while before the next project begins.

The first time I needed to hire in this way was when I sold a big market-research project to analyze different e-commerce platforms for a potential investor. Part of the job was listing hundreds of products on the Indian equivalents of eBay and then analyzing the responses. Just listing and tracking the responses alone would have taken hundreds of hours, and I only had a couple of weeks. So I subcontracted to some software engineers who could automate the process for me. This way, I could just focus on analyzing the data once it came in. Sometimes, freelancers sell the project first and then realize they need help completing it. Other times, freelancers organize in collectives or groups to sell bigger projects they will complete together. These groups of freelancers often don't take the step of formally coming together as a company. Instead, each person manages their own freelance business separately, but the members of the group agree to assemble when there is work.[12]

TV Shows

A television show falls in the middle of the continuum for this analogy. Like a movie, there is work that can be done by many freelancers. Most of the previously described roles still apply to making a television show. The critical difference is that a movie happens one time, and a television show has many episodes, sometimes spread over multiple seasons. In this case, the need for freelancers could go in either direction. If there is great uncertainty about how long this work will last, if the hiring manager has a tight budget, or if the tasks can be done interchangeably by different people, it might be best to go with freelancers. On the other hand, if the manager needs the same people to be continuous throughout the project (like the main characters in your favorite show), they'll push for longer contracts. That length of time might nudge managers toward hiring full-time employees. Or they may just periodically extend the length of the project the freelancer is contracted to perform.

An example of work that falls in this category includes some midsize consulting firms. These firms have many full-time employees, but they may also hire freelancers when the company's workload spikes beyond what the full-time staff can reasonably handle. Once the workload returns to its normal amount, the freelancer might pause working with the consulting firm until the next big project arrives. This practice is becoming increasingly common among freelancers across industries including media, technology, and professional services.

Whether to hire full-time employees or freelance services for this kind of work will depend on the manager's personal preferences. The ongoing nature of the work and the importance of having the same person doing it will likely impact their decision. If there is a lot of work and continuity is important to the manager, they'll usually prefer a full-time person. They may also prefer a full-time worker if the manager is skeptical of freelancers' skill sets or commitment to the project. If there is less work, or if it's less disruptive when the manager has to replace a person, then freelancing might be their preference. Managers may also dance between these options. For example, if the person they want to work with strongly prefers to do so as an independent worker, allowing them to freelance will help the company retain the worker. On the other hand, managers who are not sure what type of worker they want might "audition" freelancers for a full-time role by working with them on a freelance basis and then extending a full-time offer if they are happy with the outcome.

Streaming Platforms

The final category, at the opposite end of the spectrum, is the least freelancer-friendly. These projects are not a single movie or an ongoing television show but are a larger hub that creates both. In this analogy, you might think of streaming platforms like Netflix. This platform creates original content, which can be movies or television shows. It is also in a business that's driven by subscriptions to the service as a whole, which may offer other things entirely, like short content or the ability to show other people's movies and shows. This platform is also a very large company with thousands of employees, stock that is publicly listed, and a ranking in the Fortune 500.

Because these companies are so large, they have a wide variety of projects in progress at any given time, which will include a mix of both the movie and television show examples we discussed. Some subprojects may need the mostly freelance workers of movie productions; others will be better suited to the blend of freelancers and full-time employees for TV shows. There is, though, a third category of work for the large companies that is generally done by full-time employees. This work generally consists of coordinating the various subprojects the company creates, maintaining the company, and growing it as a whole. Because of the ongoing nature of this work, companies tend to prefer full-time staff for these roles, which historically also included senior leadership of the company.

This situation may be changing, however. To attract high-quality talent, some companies are finding that they have to allow their executives to also be freelancers—all the way up to the C-Suite. There has been a recent rise in "fractional" executives, ranging from chief financial officer to chief marketing officer, chief information officer, and more.[13] These leaders are considered "fractional" because they do not work full-time at any one company. Splitting their time between different companies benefits the employer, who can get high-quality talent for—you guessed it—a fraction of the price that a full-time employee would cost. The company can save on salary, as well as health insurance, sick leave, vacation pay, and other benefits. Fractionalized work may also benefit freelancers who prefer being independent to enjoy more autonomy and, in some cases, higher compensation than they would in a single full-time role.[14] As the lines between full-time and freelance blur, we can expect more acceptance of the freelance skill set, more flexible work configurations, and more cross-pollination of ideas from workers in multiple companies and industries.

GRAY AREAS

There is an ethical gray area on both sides of the company–worker relationship. Many companies with the ability to hire full-time workers choose not to because doing so would be expensive. The classic example of this is Uber, which has fought for years to keep its workers classified as independent contractors rather than employees. By using independent workers, the company avoided giving the drivers benefits or pay drivers when they didn't have passengers. While Uber is the most infamous example, companies across many industries are filling what could be full-time positions with freelancers. In journalism, for example, it is common to keep writers as freelancers, even though many might prefer to go full-time. At its extreme, this practice can become exploitative by serving the company's interests while endangering its workers'.

Some workers have also noticed an opportunity to benefit from their jobs' lenient policies. A cluster of workers who call themselves "overemployed" emerged during the pandemic, when their jobs went remote.[15] These overemployed workers chose not to freelance or have side hustles but to actually take on a second full-time job without quitting (or informing?) their existing company. Doing work for two companies secretly can lead to both reputational and legal trouble, as we saw in chapter 10.

Yet for some, overemployment is their best option for survival. One woman was left with steep medical bills after her son died.[16] Paying off those bills meant she would not be able to pay for her surviving son to attend college. When she was recruited for and offered a second job in her field, overemployment was a welcome relief. She could now comfortably pay back the medical debt, buy food, and feel at ease about her financial future. For others, overemployment is more optional, but they see it as a way to use their time productively, reclaim their independence, and secure their futures.

There will always be a spectrum of how much each side can consider the other's interests, but I hope that in the future these two sides—employers and workers—will meet near the middle. We can build toward an environment where workers in limited capacities will also get benefits and some semblance of the security they crave, and where workers in full-time capacities have more flexibility to take on other projects.

MANAGING FREELANCERS

Why does a freelancer need to know how to manage other freelancers? Three reasons. First, as we explored in chapter 9, if your freelancing business grows to a certain point, you will likely need to outsource some tasks in order to spend time on the things you are best at. For example, if you are a writer, you might hire someone to build your website. If you build websites for a living, you might find an accountant to help with your taxes, and so on. Frequently these people will be freelancers themselves. The second reason to learn how to manage freelancers arises if you take a corporate job. You may find yourself in the position of figuring out whether aspects of the company's work would be better suited to contractors or a full-time hire—having freelanced, a topic you are especially qualified to provide an opinion on. This leads to the third reason freelancers should know how to manage other freelancers. While freelancing is growing in popularity, many managers of freelancers have not actually freelanced themselves. This disparity means that you might know better than your client how to improve the relationship and unlock the best work product possible while you are still freelancing.

Let's begin by exploring two layers to freelancer management. First, how do you get the work done in a way that leaves both parties satisfied? Second, how can you go beyond that by tapping into the freelancer's superpowers?

In terms of getting the work done, managing freelancers is a lot like managing other employees. The key differences are that the freelancer you oversee may have other clients and priorities, is separated from the team, and is not on your payroll. Recognizing that freelancers have their own businesses and highly value their autonomy, you may find that they perform best when given clear expectations and then the freedom to complete the project.[17]

It will also be to your benefit to tackle the natural separation between freelancers and the rest of the team. Better communication will help you understand both sides' motivations and goals. Ravi Mishra, who managed a team of freelancers, told me, "I've tried to cultivate relationships. And then people feel more safe to say, 'Oh, I'm thinking about leaving in a few months' [and explain what they have going on]. This gives me some time to find someone, because losing a freelancer can be disruptive."[18]

Ravi is quick to caution that this approach is not freelance-specific: "It's just regular management." What *is* freelance-specific is the fact that the freelancer is not integrated in the team and often not included in company team-building events and messaging channels. Changing that, by including your freelancers in at least some of these places, can foster information flow throughout the company and create a better working relationship across the board for many years to come.[19] Having a closer relationship can also help both parties get feedback about what worked and what needed improvement, and this insight can lead to more growth and satisfaction in the long run.[20] Finally, since freelancers are not on your payroll, a best practice is to pay them promptly when they invoice. Don't make your freelancers follow up for months across every messaging platform.

Getting the work done well is the bare minimum. The bigger question is, if freelancers bring all the superpowers described throughout this book, how can managers use their freelancers more effectively to tap into this rich source of expertise? Too often, companies have a narrow view of what they want a freelancer to do and just plug them in to a predefined project. Consider taking a step back and asking the freelancer for strategic or market insight, since the freelancer is on the front lines of the industry, pitching to new clients, and observing new trends. Tommy Walker, a content strategy consultant, writes that freelancers often have a broader view of the industry than their own clients. These clients do themselves a disservice by giving freelancers narrowly scoped assignments without also asking for the freelancers' perspective on the market as a whole.[21] Consider, then, giving bigger projects when you find the right freelancers. And if you feel that your team is stagnating, explore whether adding freelancers might inject a richness of information and experience to shake up your company.

Integrating these additional and diverse perspectives into the team can allow for a better exchange of ideas and more innovation.[22] Sociologists Brian Uzzi and Jarrett Spiro find that collaborating with new partners allowed innovators to borrow concepts from one discipline, where they are standard, and apply them to a second discipline, where they are seen as creative.[23] By analyzing successful and unsuccessful Broadway musicals, researchers found that the most successful creative collaborations involved a mix of people who had worked together before with those who had not.[24] Fluidly shifting between organizations, disciplines, and teams was found to be especially useful for generating creativity.[25] Freelancers have these experiences in multiple domains, both from wearing multiple hats to run their own business and from plugging into projects for many different clients. When their experience collides with that of full-time workers, you've created fertile ground for innovation. This the heart of the freelance mindset and the reason that hiring people with a freelance background can be so powerful for any business.

Your journey into the freelance mindset has transformed you. Whether you choose to stay in the freelance world or prioritize full-time work, you take the lessons you have discovered along the way. People who don't freelance may not fully understand the range of skills and accomplishments freelancers bring to the table, so your firsthand experience in building your business and wearing every hat needed to make it run is a precious asset that you can share with others. And if you find yourself in the position of needing to advocate for yourself or another freelancer, this depth and range of experience can help you make that case. We explored different models for hiring freelance work and the best practices for managing freelancers and unleashing their specific talents. In the next section, we'll explore the future of freelancing as a whole.

SUMMARY

- Market your freelance experience to potential clients or employers by emphasizing the entrepreneurial, leadership, and creative aspects of running your own solo business.
- Understanding how managers think about hiring freelancers for onetime, repeated, or continuous work can help you position yourself to be hired for larger and more stable projects.
- Freelancers are experts on how to best work with freelancers. Use your experience to close the gap between managers and freelancers by identifying freelance-friendly projects and opportunities for connection.

12

THE FREELANCER'S FUTURE

The early days of the circus, back in the late nineteenth century, were nothing short of dazzling. Entire towns would stop work to watch in awe while the circus company set up its tents and launched a team of performers into death-defying stunts. Over time, the circus became big business. In the twentieth century, one small Iowa show became a railroad touring company and eventually an international conglomerate, as Ringling Brothers merged with Barnum & Bailey and was later bought by Mattel, the toy company famous for making Barbie and Hot Wheels. "The Greatest Show on Earth" eventually brought in more than $1 billion of revenue per year.[1]

Fast-forward to today, and the big-circus spectacle looks different. The circus rarely—if ever—comes to town. When it does, people hardly bat an eye. As we saw earlier, instead of working for a large and bureaucratic organization, David Dimitri runs his own one-man circus where he performs all the roles himself. Scores of other highly trained circus performers have also migrated from big touring companies to social media.[2] We now watch snippets of their solo performances from the isolation of our own screens instead of gathering in community with the rest of the townspeople. Our collective nostalgia for the circus of yore is tarnished by its controversial treatment of performers, both human and animal.

What lessons does the rise and fall of the circus hold for freelancers? One important lesson is that the circus failed to keep up with the needs of its workers and its audience. Today's companies likewise cannot afford to take for granted their ability to attract and retain talented workers. The gatekeepers of the past have disappeared. Now anyone can start their own circus online with just a working camera and an internet connection. This is good news for audiences. Although the circus has declined, the entertainment industry has flourished into a menu of seemingly endless choices that can satisfy every palate on earth. The absence of gatekeepers is also good for workers. To compete in such a crowded field, companies must take better care of their talent. After all, the work of entertaining did not die with Ringling Brothers' faltering balance sheet. The show may change, but it will nevertheless go on.

Our working lives are similarly on the brink of transformation. We as a society are deeply questioning what our personal and professional futures should hold. The movement toward freelancing fits neatly into our collective reimagining of a future where we have more freedom. We long to choose which projects we work on and where we do this work. We crave the ability to carve up our time and attend to the full range of our needs, from financial to the deeply personal. The freelance movement coincides with several other movements: the gradual decentralization of our financial systems and other organizations, a shift toward multi-careerism, and the departure of a large swath of the population from unsatisfactory hierarchical employment to situations where people can manage themselves.

This unique moment of reflection will have long-term repercussions. We will not have the same relationship with corporate America that we once did. The nine-to-five is no longer the only acceptable way to work. In the same way that entertainment exploded into infinite options, so too will we have radical flexibility in configuring our working lives.

But before we can fully unlock the power of freelancing, there are a few barriers that we, as a society, need to confront. These obstacles threaten our ability to make freelancing a viable career option available to everyone who wants it. Freelancers face physical, psychological, and social roadblocks. Let's explore current and future ways to address each in turn.

SUPPORTING PHYSICAL WELL-BEING

Ask a potential freelancer what holds them back from freelancing full-time, and you will often hear concerns about health insurance and the lack of a steady paycheck. Both these concerns threaten the freelancer's survival on a bodily level. Earlier, we discussed strategies to manage these risks as individuals, but what can we do at a societal level to lessen their impact on freelancers as a group?

Improving freelancer access to work and benefits is a big, hairy problem that may just require an entrepreneurial solution. Let's look at the next wave of platforms that help freelancers find work. Unlike the previous generation of platforms, these are directly owned by, and built for, freelancers.

Ramita Ravi, who we met earlier, is a professional dancer and design consultant. She and her college friend Nick Silverio noticed a unique conundrum at the intersection of freelancing and being a working artist. Although the vast majority of artists are freelancers, "no one goes into an art career being equipped and prepared to be a freelancer," she said.[3] The focus, she said, is on artistic training and technique. Ramita and Nick, who is also a dancer, gave up the benefits and steady cash flow of a more traditional job to get their careers as professional dancers off the ground.

At the same time, they recognized that having the opportunity to pursue an arts career involves a good deal of privilege, since the profession rarely offers its workers financial stability. As freelance writer and theater artist Dara Silverman told me, "It's notable to mention that I come from an upper-middle-class background. I'm not in a position where I'll be unable to pay my rent, because I have a support system when I mess up. I'm lucky. . . . Knowing that I could mess up royally and not sacrifice any of my material comforts and human needs is notable."[4]

Ramita and Nick set out to create a safety net for the one hundred million freelance artists globally.[5] Their company, Artswrk, is a platform for artists to "find stability doing the work they actually trained their whole lives to do."[6] It goes beyond casting platforms to help artists take their work throughout the arts—as vocal coaches, dance teachers, photographers, videographers, and more—and turn that work into stable, recurring income.[7] Both the cofounders' personal experience with freelancing and their networks lead to a platform that is designed and optimized from the freelancers' perspective.

Entrepreneurs Gabe Luna-Ostaseski and Adam Jackson took a different approach in cofounding their company, Braintrust, to give freelancers more ownership and control over their projects. Braintrust is a network that allows talent and clients to find each other. But unlike many other freelancing platforms, their network is designed to give freelancers ownership over their careers and the Braintrust platform itself. The platform is powered by Braintrust tokens, which freelancers can earn by performing activities like bidding on projects, getting high ratings from clients, taking online classes, and inviting both freelancers and clients to the network.[8] Holding more Braintrust tokens unlocks different benefits in the network. Importantly, each token also represents one vote on how Braintrust should be governed. The more Braintrust tokens you have, the greater your say in how it's run. Conceptually, Braintrust turns all its freelancers into owners of the platform. You could think of it as a twist on worker cooperatives—on a global scale.

In addition to reimagining freelance platforms, entrepreneurs are also tackling the challenge of providing health insurance and other benefits to a decentralized or fragmented workforce. Both Artswrk and Braintrust have partnerships with start-ups that help their freelance members get better health insurance.[9] Although we are at the beginning of this new wave of freelance opportunity, the tide seems to be turning in a promising direction, which can be further supported by legislation that protects the rights of freelancers.

NOURISHING PSYCHOLOGICAL HEALTH

The preceding entrepreneurial and policy solutions can help freelancers survive, but what needs to be done to help them thrive? The trend toward freelancing coincides with unprecedented rates of burnout, depression, anxiety, and other mental health challenges on a societal scale. While we can hardly say there is a direct relationship between freelancing and such widespread malaise, we do know that for now freelancers are largely expected to battle each of these mental health threats alone. Let's examine how we can help freelancers take better care of their psychological health.

Making therapy accessible is an important first step. So far, free mental health resources cluster around two ends of a spectrum: One is the beginning of a mental health journey, where most social media content focuses as influencers introduce concepts and share useful reminders. The other extreme is defusing a moment of crisis—like preventing a suicide—which is where government-funded hotlines focus. Both are affordable and relatively easy to access, but they miss out on the wide swath of freelancers with experiences somewhere between those two extremes. Companies like BetterHelp and Talkspace have made care for this middle group cheaper, with virtual and text message options, but it can still be too costly for many freelancers, who may see it as a luxury purchase in light of unpredictable income. Until we have more widely available group therapy, subsidies, and improved insurance access, there are things we can do to make existing offerings more effective. By normalizing honest conversations about mental health, sharing resources, and examining our own contributions to hustle culture and the expectations of 24/7 responsiveness, we can collectively create more sustainable working practices for one another.

CREATING A FREELANCING COMMUNITY

Freelancing can be a lonely journey.[10] Isolation was a common theme in my conversations with freelancers. Without a community, you also miss the human connection and free flow of information that both validates your problems and helps you find solutions. How else can you find out if you are being paid fairly, for example, without knowing other freelancers' rates? And how can you find work without knowing where people are looking for your skill set? Creating space for freelancers to find connection and community will improve our collective health, problem-solving, creativity, focus, trust, networks, and lifestyle.

So far, the burden to create community has been on the individual freelancers who feel lonely, but in recent years, more businesses are noticing this market need and opportunity. Creating more opportunities for casual networking, like the type you might do at a conference, was a central design principle when coworking spaces were first designed. For example, WeWork's office floor plan was optimized to give people the maximum number of chances to bump into one another, such as when taking the elevator or grabbing a coffee.[11] In-person coworking was a great first step in tackling the isolation of being self-employed.

Not all freelancers are able or interested in commuting to a physical office to do their individual work. For those folks, virtual coworking platforms provide a great alternative. In fact, the vast majority of this book was written in two online coworking spaces: Focusmate and Shut Up & Write. In both, you join virtual productivity sessions with one or more people. You tell each other your goals for the session, possibly make some chitchat, and then wish each other good luck before working silently together until the designated time has elapsed. Afterward, you tell each other how you fared, and the session ends. Similar virtual tribes sprouted up to take classes, share hobbies, or even play games.

Interactions with relative strangers might seem like a strange antidote to freelance isolation, but in addition to providing a brief boost of connection and productivity, they can provide a host of professional rewards. In a landmark 1973 paper, Stanford sociologist Mark Granovetter refers to these more casual relationships as "weak ties."[12] Your weak ties include your acquaintances, people you see every so often, and others you've never met but have something in common with you (e.g., going to the same school). Our weak ties can offer new opportunities, including jobs.[13]

One challenge with casual connections is that you may not always be able to ask them for advice with your professional challenges. If you don't have access to a community you can discuss your challenges with, some freelancers suggest turning to podcasts. One freelancer told me she found a podcast that was essentially a "failure lab": "There was a bunch of people talking about their epic fails. At the time, that's what I needed to hear. I don't need to hear Jack Dorsey talking about how he won the Twitter game. That is not inspirational for me right now."[14] Instead, hearing people talk openly about their challenges and what went wrong was reassuring to her. Of freelancing she said: "It helped me persevere and figure out why I wanted to keep doing this. That in itself is a privilege."[15]

As freelancing becomes more widespread, my hope is that we will find new solutions to reduce loneliness. Perhaps, we already are.

A wave of entrepreneurial, social, and policy efforts are striving to improve what it means to be a worker, informed by the freelance perspective. While there are still many open questions about how we as a society can and should work, we have a shot at creating a better world. In this new world, both the workers who have nine-to-fives and those who have less-structured jobs would enjoy good health care, a safety net when sick, the ability to take a vacation without fear of lost income, the sense of thriving in work and life, and the feeling of belonging to a community. Together, we can blend the best of both freelance and full-time experiences to make this new world a reality, and bring more freedom to the way each of us works, plays, and lives.

SUMMARY

- To truly unlock our potential as a society, freelancers need better access to benefits and community.
- A mix of entrepreneurial and policy solutions are being developed by and for freelancers.
- The shift to a society where we can all follow our dreams and pay our bills begins with you.

CONCLUSION

As a child, when I wanted to be a detective, an artist, and a lawyer, I always thought I'd have to choose just one. I never imagined a world where having three careers was possible. And neither did my dad when he told me that a career other than law was too risky. He was trying to help me find a field where I could get work no matter what happened in the world.

At the same time, my dad's career was more complicated than the advice he gave me. He repeatedly left the stable and familiar world behind—first, as an immigrant; later, by alternating between full-time jobs and self-employment. He longed to follow his own path, in spite of the risks. I now realize we were grappling with the same question: How can you combine the stability of traditional employment with the rush of working on something that is your own?

There isn't a single answer, but with the freelance mindset we open a world of new possibilities. In this world, if you want to be a detective, an artist, and a lawyer, you can. Maybe you work full-time as a detective, teach part-time at a law school, and submit your work to art festivals each year. Or perhaps you're a full-time artist who consults on detective cases and dusts off your JD to look over the occasional contract. Or maybe you walk a different path entirely.

The beauty of a freelance mindset is that instead of choosing one job, you can choose the combination of careers and hobbies that works best for you.

Whether you're a seasoned freelancer, midway through your journey, or just getting started, you have a lot to celebrate! You've made a leap of faith into the unfamiliar world of freelancing, engaged with its challenges head-on, and emerged triumphant. You've gained more mastery over two vastly different worlds: the solo career and corporate employment. And since you have the skills to navigate both worlds, you can custom-build a career that feels right for you.

This journey has transformed you, putting you in a powerful position to further yourself and bring other freelancers along. Your new mindset will shift your behavior, tangibly changing how you spend your time, interact with people, and structure your career. Like water that ripples outward when a single pebble is tossed into a pond, your new way of living will influence your friends' ways of life, which will then influence the community's. When we all shift our mindsets together, we have a movement that can create a better way of working and living for everyone. And this movement begins with you.

ACKNOWLEDGMENTS

Book writing, like freelancing, might seem like a solitary journey. In reality, it has taken an entire community to bring *The Freelance Mindset* to life. I'm so grateful to all of the following people for making this book possible.

Thank you to my wonderful agent, April Eberhardt, for believing in me when I had just a tiny seed of an idea, championing me throughout the entire process, and helping this book find a home with Suzanne Staszak-Silva. Thank you, Suzanne, and the rest of the Rowman & Littlefield team: Tricia Currie-Knight, Joanna Wattenberg, Alyssa Hawkins, Paulette Baker, Susan Hershberg, and Arc Indexing. You've been a dream to work with. I'm forever grateful you took a chance on me.

A small but tireless army helped me turn this tiny idea into something tangible. Thank you, Patricia Boyd, for your impeccable attention to detail with thorough and speedy developmental edits; Katie Bannon, for improving my prose and helping me blast through blocks in the writing process; Kristan Sargeant, for helping me find my voice and feel empowered to share it with the world; Tanaya Raj, for enthusiastically creating beautiful illustrations that bring the book to life; Megan Posco, for helping this book find its audience; and Shalene Gupta, for spending hours upon hours teaching me to interview, helping me refine my ideas, editing my drafts, and providing moral support over coffee and salads. Okay, fine, I mean pastries.

I'm beyond grateful to April Rinne, John Kador, Gorick Ng, and Eliza VanCort for helping me find the path forward, both as a freelancer and as a writer.

There would be no freelance mindset without the many people who generously shared their insights about freelancing in interviews with me. Though I could not include all your stories, I am deeply grateful for your perspectives. Thank you to Cara Barone, Chelsea Lorraine, Connor Swenson, Dan Pinnolis, Danielle Langton, Dara Silverman, David Dimitri, Diony Cespedes, Divya Chhabra, Erin Levi, Ernesto Valverde, Erwin Felicilda, Gabe Luna-Ostaseki, Gabe Peyton, Jason Jhung, Jim Gallant, John Choi, Jordan Hayles, Josue Tovar, Kareem Khubchandani, Kayla Gray, Kevin Chiu, Kristan Sargeant, Kristen Powell, Lalita Ballesteros, Magaly Colimon-Christopher, Manya Chyslinski, Marah Paley, Matthew Huff, Max Fucci, Moira MacDonald, Nancy Zuo, Natasha Mehra, Nate Garrido, Nick Adler, Paul Millerd, Ramita Ravi, Rose Lake, Sally Collings, Sarabeth Burke, Saumya Dave, Svetlana Grigoreva, Tamala Baldwin, and Vyjayanthi Vadrevu, as well as those whose names appeared elsewhere or who wished to remain anonymous.

Thank you to everyone who has ever hired me, whether freelance or full-time. You've changed my life.

Ian Lee, Will Papper, and my incredible colleagues at Syndicate, past and present: I am honored to get to work with you and so grateful to be part of a company that supports its employees following their dreams. Thank you, Adam Lukasik, Alex Zandi, Aman Puri, Blake Johnston, Carlo Berdejo, Conner Swenberg, Delleon McGlone, Gustavo Guimaraes, Iman Bright, Isaac Bremseth, James Robinson, James Seely, Jenn Kalidoss, Jeremy Wei, Jihad Esmail, Jordan Pappas, Justin Ridgely, Keenan Monroe, Kevin Huo, Luis Clague, Nathan Hausman, Nicole Blystone, Nikki Kiga, Oliver Qin, Sida Li, Tony DiPadova, and Yang You for constantly inspiring me.

Thank you to Eyal Markovich, Uri Klarman, Aleksandar Kuzmanovic, Eleni Steinman, Yaara Lavi, Dan Blahut, Greg Richards, Jeff Marowits, Seyla Azoz, Julia Henkels, Peps Bengzon, Rishi Malhotra, Vinodh Bhat, Hiba Irshad, Gina Safdar, Mahesh Narayanan, Benjamin Zilnicki, Carissa Biggie, Dana Baron, Judy Shandling, Laura Englehardt, Marco Frigeri, Terry Mullins, and many more for being extraordinarily kind and instructive colleagues.

To the thousands of classmates and teachers who have taught and encouraged me along the way, I am so grateful to you for helping me grow into the person I am today. Thank you to the Harvard Business School Women in Consulting alumni virtual group, including Kathy Murray, Heather Myers, Betty Ng, Lisa Argette Ahmad, Ricky Surie,

Shaifali Aggarwal, Susan Meier, and Brooke Alexander Yakin, for showing me the ropes as a self-employed consultant. And thank you to the Two Ten Footwear Foundation and Steve Nichols for helping me afford higher education. I hope I've made you proud.

Support from the virtual world helped bring this book into the physical world. GrubStreet, thank you for your online classes and annual Muse and the Marketplace conference, where I learned to write a book proposal and met many of my collaborators. To my fellow writers at Shut Up & Write, thank you for motivating me every day and for supporting me through all the ups and downs of the writing process. My virtual coworking friends, Selin Öker, Kristen Augustine, and Sarra Lev, thank you for working by my side as we conquered our deadlines together.

Some of my clearest thinking happened while dancing. Thank you to the teachers whose patience and positivity uplifted my days: Finis Jhung, Ai Toyoshima, Mayumi Omagari, Swarali Karulkar, Sahasra Sambamoorthi, Sierra Powell, Rohit Gijare, Ayesha Khanna, Pooja Narang, Tony Guerrero, Inna Kuznetsova, Karen Arceneaux, and many more.

For their friendship, endless encouragement, and help reviewing my incredibly rough drafts, I am eternally grateful to Patty Martins, Victoria Lee, Erika Todd, Gaayatry Para, Mainak Ghosh, T. T. Nguyen Duc, Samyukta Mullangi, Ritu Tandon, Rabeea Khan, Eric Chianese, and Amrit Dhir. I also thank Prabhakar Reddy, Ravi Mishra, Sandy Danh, Pooja Patnaik, Lilly Beshore, Catie Bennett, Jonathan Pride, Ankita Jangir, Monika Thangalapalli, Monica Nanani, Dinesh Reddy, Anushree Sreedhar, Jyot Bawa, Ebele Mora, Marisa Taney, Ravi Chachra, Vikram Chachra, Alan Sun, Tiff Zarrella, Drew Eramo, and countless others for keeping me inspired, laughing, and moving forward throughout the long writing process.

For anyone I wasn't able to include in these pages: *thank you*. Please know that my gratitude far exceeds my rusty memory.

Thank you to my family near and far. I am so grateful for the love and support you've given me throughout the years. Mom and Dad, I can't thank you enough for everything you have given me, but I will always try. I love you.

Last but not least, dear reader, I am grateful for you! Thank you for spending some of your precious time with me.

NOTES

INTRODUCTION

1. Joseph Campbell, *The Hero with a Thousand Faces* (New York: Pantheon Books, 1949); Maureen Murdock, *The Heroine's Journey*, 1st ed. (Boston: Shambhala, 1990); Victoria Lynn Schmidt, *45 Master Characters: Mythic Models for Creating Original Characters* (Writer's Digest Books, 2012).

CHAPTER 1

1. David Dimitri, interview with the author, March 22, 2022.
2. "About," David Dimitri, accessed May 6, 2022, http://daviddimitri.ch/performing-artist-and-high-wire-walker.
3. Some details of David Dimitri's story come from Roger Catlin, "The High Wire of Going It Alone in 'One Man Circus,'" *Washington Post*, June 27, 2019, sec. Theater & Dance, www.washingtonpost.com/goingoutguide/theater-dance/the-high-wire-of-going-it-alone-in-one-man-circus/2019/06/26/15b0dd64-961c-11e9-830a-21b9b36b64ad_story.html. Thank you, Roger, for letting me use David's story to illustrate the transformation many people make in going from a traditional employment model to a freelance mindset!
4. Dimitri, interview with the author.
5. Catlin, "The High Wire of Going It Alone in 'One Man Circus.'"
6. Dimitri, interview with the author.
7. Catlin, "The High Wire of Going It Alone in 'One Man Circus.'"
8. "About," L'homme Cirque, accessed April 18, 2022, www.lhommecirque.com/The_One_Man_Circus/One_Man_Circus/About.html; Dimitri, interview with the author.
9. Dimitri, interview with the author.

10. Name has been changed at interviewee's request.

11. Josue Tovar, interview with the author, May 29, 2022.

12. For hourly earnings, mental health and well-being, see "Freelance Forward 2020," Upwork, September 2020, www.upwork.com/documents/freelance-forward-2020. For flexibility, see Adam Ozimek, "Freelance Forward Economist Report," Upwork, 2021, www.upwork.com/research/freelance-forward-2021.

13. Name has been changed.

14. Ernesto Valverde, interview with the author, December 30, 2021.

15. Chelsea Lorraine, interview with the author, May 25, 2022.

16. John Kador, interview with the author, December 24, 2021

17. Divya Chhabra, interview with the author, May 25, 2022

18. Sir Walter Scott, *Ivanhoe*, 1819

19. "The Surprising History of 'Freelance,'" Merriam-Webster, accessed May 29, 2022, www.merriam-webster.com/words-at-play/freelance-origin-meaning.

20. David Lurie, "Graduate Job Seeking: The Rise of the 'Slasher,'" *The Guardian*, February 1, 2011, sec. Guardian Careers, www.theguardian.com/careers/careers-blog/graduate-job-seeking-the-rise-of-the-slasher; Emma Gannon, *The Multi-Hyphen Life* (Kansas City: Andrews McMeel Publishing, 2020).

21. "Aristotle," History, accessed April 19, 2022, www.history.com/topics/ancient-history/aristotle.

22. "Imhotep," *World History Encyclopedia*, February 16, 2016, www.worldhistory.org/imhotep/.

23. "Zhang Heng," in *New World Encyclopedia*, accessed April 19, 2022, www.newworldencyclopedia.org/entry/Zhang_Heng.

24. Michael Deakin, "Hypatia," *Britannica*, February 25, 2022, www.britannica.com/biography/Hypatia.

CHAPTER 2

1. The movie is based on the semi-autobiographical play of the same name by Jonathan Larson.

2. Quote from Lin-Manuel Miranda, *Tick, Tick . . . BOOM!*, based on the stage musical of the same title, written by Jonathan Larson (Netflix, 2021).

3. Vyjayanthi Vadrevu, interview with the author, December 23, 2021.

4. Vadrevu, edited slightly for clarity.

5. Jason Jhung, interview with the author, December 24, 2021.

6. Jhung, "How Much Does a Medial Collateral Ligament (MCL) Repair Cost Near Me?" MDsave, accessed April 16, 2022, www.mdsave.com/procedures/medial-collateral-ligament-mcl-repair/d78bf8c8.

7. Saumya Dave, interview with the author, May 24, 2022.

8. "Supplemental Data Measuring the Effects of the Coronavirus (COVID-19) Pandemic on the Labor Market," US Bureau of Labor Statistics, April 5, 2022, www.bls.gov/cps/effects-of-the-coronavirus-covid-19-pandemic.htm; Heather Long, "U.S. Now Has 22 Million Unemployed, Wiping out a Decade of Job Gains," *Washington Post*, April 26, 2020, www.washingtonpost.com/business/2020/04/16/unemployment-claims-coronavirus.

9. Jon Younger, "The Coronavirus Pandemic Is Driving Huge Growth in Remote Freelance Work," *Forbes*, March 29, 2020, www.forbes.com/sites/jonyounger/2020/03/29/this-pandemic-is-driving-huge-growth-in-remote-freelance-work.

10. Tamala Baldwin, interview with the author, May 31, 2022.

11. Charles B. Handy, *The Age of Unreason*, 1st ed. (Boston: Harvard Business School Press, 1989).

12. Divya Chhabra, interview with the author.

CHAPTER 3

1. Finis Jhung, *Ballet for Life: A Pictorial Memoir* (Ballet Dynamics, Inc., 2018), 26, 164, 184, 190.

2. Jhung, *Ballet for Life*, 194.

3. Name has been changed at interviewee's request.

4. Kristan Sargeant, interview with the author, December 27, 2021.

5. Erin Levi, interview with the author, June 4, 2022.

6. Moira MacDonald, interview with the author, December 21, 2021.

7. Matthew Huff, interview with the author, December 27, 2021.

8. April Rinne, *Flux: 8 Superpowers for Thriving in Constant Change* (Berrett-Koehler Publishers, 2021).

9. Chua, Hannah Faye, Julie E. Boland, and Richard E. Nisbett. "Cultural variation in eye movements during scene perception." *Proceedings of the National Academy of Sciences* 102, no. 35 (2005): 12629–12633.

10. American Psychological Association, "Stress in America™ 2021: Stress and Decision-Making during the Pandemic," 2021, 3, www.apa.org/news/press/releases/stress/2021/decision-making-october-2021.pdf. Forty-nine percent of American adults surveyed responded that "the coronavirus pandemic has made planning for their future feel impossible."

11. American Psychological Association, 3.

12. Dalai Lama XIV Bstan-'dzin-rgya-mtsho and Desmond Tutu, *The Book of Joy: Lasting Happiness in a Changing World* (New York: Avery, 2016). In the

West, remembering one's own mortality is known as memento mori and can be traced back thousands of years. See, for example, Epictetus, *The Enchiridion*, trans. Elizabeth Carter, The Internet Classics Archive, 135 CE, http://classics.mit.edu/Epictetus/epicench.html.

13. Lodro Rinzler, *The Buddha Walks into a Bar—: A Guide to Life for a New Generation*, 1st ed. (Boston: Shambhala, 2012).

14. Pema Chödrön, "Three Methods for Working with Chaos," Lion's Roar, January 20, 2022, www.lionsroar.com/pema-chodrons-three-methods-for-working-with-chaos/. This article is excerpted from Pema Chodron, *When Things Fall Apart: Heart Advice for Difficult Times* (Shambhala Classics, 1996).

15. Finis Jhung, interview with the author, December 22, 2021; Jhung, *Ballet for Life*.

16. Jhung, interview with the author, December 22, 2021; Kador, interview with the author; Huff, interview with the author; Manya Chylinski, interview with the author, December 27, 2021.

17. Jhung, interview with the author, December 22, 2021.

18. Jhung.

CHAPTER 4

1. *Brown Girl Magazine*, "Slashie // Summit 2019," IFundWomen, accessed March 27, 2022, https://ifundwomen.com/projects/slashie-summit-2019.

2. Sarabeth Berk, interview with the author, January 10, 2022.

3. Berk.

4. Mihaly Csikszentmihalyi, *Flow: The Psychology of Optimal Experience*, 1st ed. (New York: Harper & Row, 1990).

5. Julia Cameron, *The Artist's Way: 25th Anniversary Edition*, 10th ed. (TarcherPerigee, 2002).

6. Berk, interview with the author.

7. Kristan Sargeant, interview with the author.

8. Laura Oliver, "Is This Japanese Concept the Secret to a Long, Happy, Meaningful Life?" World Economic Forum, August 9, 2017, www.weforum.org/agenda/2017/08/is-this-japanese-concept-the-secret-to-a-long-life/; Marc Winn, "What Is Your *Ikigai*?" *The View Inside Me* (blog), May 14, 2014, https://theviewinside.me/what-is-your-ikigai/#comments.

9. Abraham Harold Maslow, "A Theory of Human Motivation," *Psychological Review* 50, no. 4 (1943): 370.

10. "Value of 1971 US Dollars Today—Inflation Calculator," Inflation Tool, accessed March 28, 2022, www.inflationtool.com/us-dollar/1971-to-present-value.

11. Edward Deci, "The Effects of Externally Mediated Rewards on Intrinsic Motivation," *Journal of Personality and Social Psychology* 18 (April 1, 1971): 105–15, https://doi.org/10.1037/h0030644.

12. Shalene Gupta, interview with the author, December 28, 2021.

13. Nicholas Hytner, *Center Stage* (Columbia Pictures, 2000).

14. "How Did Vincent van Gogh Become Famous after His Death?" Van Gogh Museum, accessed July 10, 2022, www.vangoghmuseum.nl/en/art-and-stories/vincent-van-gogh-faq/how-did-van-gogh-become-famous-after-his-death.

15. Magaly Colimon-Christopher, interview with the author, January 6, 2022.

16. KJ Dell'Antonia, "How High School Ruined Leisure," *New York Times*, May 18, 2019, sec. Opinion, www.nytimes.com/2019/05/18/opinion/sunday/college-admissions-extracurriculars.html.

17. Huff, interview with the author.

18. Steven M. Gelber, *Hobbies: Leisure and the Culture of Work in America* (Columbia University Press, 1999), 24.

19. Maria Popova, "How Einstein Thought: Why 'Combinatory Play' Is the Secret of Genius," *The Marginalian* (blog), August 14, 2013, www.themarginalian.org/2013/08/14/how-einstein-thought-combinatorial-creativity.

20. Mark S. Granovetter, "The Strength of Weak Ties," *The American Journal of Sociology* 78, no. 6 (May 1973): 1360–80; Laura K. Gee, Jason Jones, and Moira Burke, "Social Networks and Labor Markets: How Strong Ties Relate to Job Finding on Facebook's Social Network," *Journal of Labor Economics*, January 26, 2017, https://doi.org/10.1086/686225; Ian Leslie, "Why Your 'Weak-Tie' Friendships May Mean More than You Think," BBC, July 2, 2020, www.bbc.com/worklife/article/20200701-why-your-weak-tie-friendships-may-mean-more-than-you-think.

21. Rohit Gijare, "Reminder: Be Kind to Yourself, Take a Break," photo caption, Instagram, July 6, 2020, www.instagram.com/p/CCSVWTIl8m3. After a few weeks away, Rohit returned to dance and now enjoys a thriving teaching and performance career.

22. Rachel Zar, "What Actually Happens to Your Body When You Stop Dancing," *Dance Magazine*, May 31, 2018, www.dancemagazine.com/rest-from-exercise.

23. Inna Kuznetsova, interview with the author, May 11, 2022.

24. Marian Bull, "The Complicated Reality of Doing What You Love," Vox, August 25, 2021, www.vox.com/the-highlight/22620178/hobby-job-leisure-labor.

25. Colimon-Christopher, interview with the author.

26. Colimon-Christopher.

CHAPTER 5

1. Thanks to Marek Kosnik, Mark Michelman, Namrata Singhal, Samer Kallas, and Stephanie Swingle for this insightful conversation!

2. Ravi Mishra, interview with the author, December 28, 2021.

3. "Recession ho ya inflation, shaadiyan toh hote rahenge, na?"

4. Ramita Ravi, interview with the author, November 22, 2021.

5. James Carville and Paul Begala, *Buck Up, Suck Up . . . and Come Back When You Foul Up: 12 Winning Secrets from the War Room* (New York: Simon & Schuster, 2002).

6. www.dailymail.co.uk/news/article-5109115/Lions-big-giraffe-against-odds-epic-fight.html; www.nationalgeographic.com/animals/article/lions-attack-giraffe-in-rare-video-in-kruger-south-africa.

7. Chelsea Lorraine, interview with the author.

8. John Kador, interview with the author.

9. Kristen Powell, interview with the author, May 31, 2022.

10. Gabe Peyton, interview with the author, June 1, 2022.

11. Kayla Gray, interview with the author, December 20, 2021.

12. Tiago Forte, "The Rise of the Full-Stack Freelancer," Forte Labs, June 23, 2017, https://fortelabs.co/blog/the-rise-of-the-full-stack-freelancer.

13. Matthew Huff, interview with the author.

14. "Flywheel," in *Britannica*, accessed March 23, 2022, www.britannica.com/technology/flywheel.

15. Jim Collins, "Good to Great," October 2001, www.jimcollins.com/article_topics/articles/good-to-great.html#articletop. Excerpted from the book *Good to Great.*

CHAPTER 6

1. Thanks to Drew Eramo for being the lone Yankees fan and a wonderful friend!

2. The drought is popularly considered to have begun in 1918, which was the last time the Red Sox won the World Series until 2004. However, Babe Ruth's trade to the Yankees was completed in 1920. History.com editors, "New York Yankees Announce Purchase of Babe Ruth," in *HISTORY* (A&E Television Networks, November 16, 2009), www.history.com/this-day-in-history/new-york-yankees-announce-purchase-of-babe-ruth.

3. Amy Novotney, "The Psychology of Scarcity," American Psychological Association, February 2014, www.apa.org/monitor/2014/02/scarcity. For more on scarcity, see Sendhil Mullainathan and Eldar Shafir, *Scarcity: Why Having Too Little Means So Much*, 1st ed. (New York: Times Books, Henry Holt and Company, 2013); Stephen R. Covey, *The 7 Habits of Highly Effective People: Restoring the Character Ethic*, rev. ed. (New York: Free Press, 2004).

4. Steven F. Maier and Martin E. P. Seligman, "Learned Helplessness at Fifty: Insights from Neuroscience," *Psychological Review* 123, no. 4 (July 2016): 349–67, https://doi.org/10.1037/rev0000033.

5. Michael Clair, "The Red Sox Once Turned to a Witch to End a Losing Streak . . . and It Worked," Cut4 by MLB.Com, October 31, 2018, www.mlb.com/cut4/red-sox-ended-losing-streak-thanks-to-witch-laurie-cabot-c299743668.

6. Clair.

7. Associated Press, "Red Sox Fan Climbs Everest to Break Ruth's Curse," ESPN, June 20, 2001, sec. Baseball, www.espn.com/mlb/news/2001/0620/1216282.html.

8. Brian McGrory, "Taking Teeth Out of Curse?" *Boston Globe*, September 2, 2004, http://archive.boston.com/sports/baseball/redsox/articles/2004/09/02/taking_teeth_out_of_curse.

9. Steve Popper, "Yankees Slide to a New Low Against Indians: 22–0," *New York Times*, September 1, 2004, sec. Baseball, www.nytimes.com/2004/09/01/sports/baseball/yankees-slide-to-a-newlow-against-indians-220.html.

10. Roger Rubin, "After Babe Ruth's Curse Was Broken, Attention Has Turned to Alex Rodriguez's Failures in the Clutch," *NY Daily News*, September 20, 2009, sec. Sports, Baseball, Yankees, www.nydailynews.com/sports/baseball/yankees/babe-ruth-curse-broken-attention-turned-alex-rodriguez-failures-clutch-article-1.406032.

11. Ian Browne, "Best Season Ever? Hard to Top 2004 Red Sox," MLB.com, December 26, 2021, www.mlb.com/news/classic-seasons-2004-red-sox.

12. Browne.

13. Browne.

14. B. S. Everitt and A Skrondal, "Regression to the Mean," in *The Cambridge Dictionary of Statistics* (Cambridge, UK: Cambridge University Press, 2010).

15. John Kador, interview with the author.

16. Sally Collings, interview with the author, January 5, 2022.

17. Ernie Valverde, interview with the author, edited slightly for clarity.

18. Collings, interview with the author, edited slightly for clarity.

19. Connor Swenson, interview with the author, May 27, 2022.

20. Cara Barone, interview with the author, January 16, 2022.

21. Matthew Huff, interview with the author.

22. Knew Health and Sedera are two examples of medical cost-sharing providers. One Medical, Forward, and Parsley are examples of medical subscriptions.

23. Examples of such employers include Starbucks, Lowe's, Costco, and UPS. See "Benefits and Perks," Starbucks Coffee Company, accessed April 8, 2022, www.starbucks.com/careers/working-at-starbucks/benefits-and-perks; "Your Benefits Choices Guide," Lowe's, accessed April 8, 2022, www.myloweslife.com/lowesnet/portal/enrollments/files/Linked_PDFs/Lowes_PT_EG_PDF_Final.pdf; "Employees," Costco, March 2022, www.costco.com/sustainability-employees.html; "UPS Part-Time Benefits," TeamstersCare, May 13, 2014, www.teamsterscare.com/active-members-2/ups-part-time-benefits.

24. Diony Cespedes, January 29, 2022.

25. Coryanne Hicks, "9 Charts Showing Why You Should Invest Today," *US News*, July 23, 2018, https://money.usnews.com/investing/investing-101/articles/2018-07-23/9-charts-showing-why-you-should-invest-today.

26. "One Participant 401k Plans," Internal Revenue Service, November 8, 2021, www.irs.gov/retirement-plans/one-participant-401k-plans; "Understanding the Self-Employed 401(k)," Fidelity, accessed April 8, 2022, www.fidelity.com/learning-center/personal-finance/retirement/self-employed-401k; "Retirement Plans for Self-Employed People," Internal Revenue Service, November 15, 2021, www.irs.gov/retirement-plans/retirement-plans-for-self-employed-people; Arielle O'Shea, "What Is a Solo 401(k)? Self-Employed Retirement," NerdWallet, March 2, 2022, www.nerdwallet.com/article/investing/what-is-a-solo-401k.

27. The acronym SEP IRA stands for Simplified Employee Pension Individual Retirement Account. You can learn more at "Simplified Employee Pension Plan (SEP)," Internal Revenue Service, January 3, 2022, www.irs.gov/retirement-plans/plan-sponsor/simplified-employee-pension-plan-sep; Arielle O'Shea, "Simplified Employee Pension (SEP) IRA: How It Works," NerdWallet, March 4, 2022, www.nerdwallet.com/article/investing/what-is-a-sep-ira.

CHAPTER 7

1. The invention is attributed to both Art Fry and Spencer Silver. "History Timeline: Post-It® Notes," Post-it, US, accessed April 22, 2022, www.post-it.com/3M/en_US/post-it/contact-us/about-us.

2. Ramita Ravi, interview with the author.

3. "Protestant Ethic," in *Britannica*, accessed April 22, 2022, www.britannica.com/topic/Protestant-ethic; Oliver Burkeman, "The Protestant Work Ethic," *The Guardian*, September 10, 2010, sec. Life and style, www.theguardian.com/lifeandstyle/2010/sep/11/pain-gain-work-ethic-burkeman.

4. "What Is India's Caste System?" *BBC News*, June 19, 2019, sec. India, www.bbc.com/news/world-asia-india-35650616.

5. Elliott Zaagman, "The Future of China's Work Culture," TechCrunch, October 9, 2021, https://social.techcrunch.com/2021/10/09/the-future-of-chinas-work-culture.

6. Sarah Epstein, "4 Types of Grief Nobody Told You About," *Psychology Today*, April 17, 2019, www.psychologytoday.com/us/blog/between-the-generations/201904/4-types-grief-nobody-told-you-about.

7. Traci Bank Cohen, "Grieving the Loss of a Life You Wanted," Goop, accessed April 22, 2022, https://goop.com/wellness/relationships/grieving-the-loss-of-a-life-you-wanted.

8. Saumya Dave, Interview with the author, May 24, 2022.

9. Epstein, "4 Types of Grief Nobody Told You About."

10. Cohen, "Grieving the Loss of a Life You Wanted."

11. Scott Berinato, "That Discomfort You're Feeling Is Grief," *Harvard Business Review*, March 23, 2020, https://hbr.org/2020/03/that-discomfort-youre-feeling-is-grief; Cohen, "Grieving the Loss of a Life You Wanted."

12. David Burns, *Feeling Good: The New Mood Therapy* (HarperCollins, 2012), 327.

13. Timothy O'Brien, "When Your Job Is Your Identity, Professional Failure Hurts More," *Harvard Business Review*, June 18, 2019, https://hbr.org/2019/06/how-we-confuse-our-roles-with-our-self.

14. Larry Alton, "How Low Self-Esteem Affects Your Earning Potential," *NBC News*, November 15, 2017, sec. Better by Today, www.nbcnews.com/better/business/why-low-self-esteem-may-be-hurting-your-career-ncna814156, quoting author Barrie Davenport.

15. Burns, *Feeling Good: The New Mood Therapy*, 332–39.

16. Dawn Brown, "How To Build Your Identity in and out of Work," *Forbes*, accessed April 22, 2022, www.forbes.com/sites/forbesbusinesscouncil/2021/07/01/how-to-build-your-identity-in-and-out-of-work.

17. Marilynn B. Brewer, "The Social Self: On Being the Same and Different at the Same Time," *Personality and Social Psychology Bulletin* 17, no. 5 (October 1, 1991): 475–82.

18. Barbara Minto, *The Pyramid Principle* (Harlow: Financial Times Prentice Hall, 2001).

19. Sarabeth Berk, interview with the author.

CHAPTER 8

1. Wilma is famously quoted as saying, "My doctor told me I would never walk again. My mother told me I would. I believed my mother." Arlisha R. Norwood, "Wilma Rudolph," National Women's History Museum, 2017, www.womenshistory.org/education-resources/biographies/wilma-rudolph.

2. M. B. Roberts, "Rudolph Ran and World Went Wild," ESPN.com, accessed April 14, 2022, www.espn.com/sportscentury/features/00016444.html.

3. Shalene Gupta, interview with the author.

4. For more on the career jungle gym, see Patricia Sellers, "PowerPoint: Get Used to the Jungle Gym," *Fortune*, August 7, 2009, https://fortune.com/2009/08/07/power-point-get-used-to-the-jungle-gym/; Sheryl Sandberg and Nell Scovell, *Lean in: Women, Work, and the Will to Lead* (London: WH Allen, 2015).

5. For career lattice, see Andy Przystanski, "What Is a Career Lattice?" Lattice, September 11, 2020, https://lattice.com/library/what-is-a-career-lattice. For infinite set of pipes, see Bel Pesce, *5 Ways to Kill Your Dreams*, TEDGlobal, 2014, www.ted.com/talks/bel_pesce_5_ways_to_kill_your_dreams/transcript. For squiggly career, see Helen Tupper and Sarah Ellis, *The Squiggly Career: Ditch the Ladder, Discover Opportunity, Design Your Career* (Penguin Business, 2020).

6. Victoria Lee, interview with the author, November 9, 2021.

7. Natasha Mehra, interview with the author, December 17, 2021.

8. Charles B. Handy, *The Age of Unreason*, 1st ed. (Boston: Harvard Business School Press, 1989); David Lurie, "Graduate Job Seeking: The Rise of the 'Slasher,'" *The Guardian*, February 1, 2011, sec. Guardian Careers, www.theguardian.com/careers/careers-blog/graduate-job-seeking-the-rise-of-the-slasher.

9. The term "slashies" derives from the "slasher" careers, a description coined in Marci Alboher, *One Person/Multiple Careers: A New Model for Work/Life Success* (New York: Warner Business Books, 2007). It was later popularized as "slashies" by news outlets such as *The Guardian* and *Brown Girl Magazine*. The term "multihyphenates" has been used informally since the 1970s to describe celebrities with multiple professions. It was popularized and brought to the

mainstream by Emma Gannon, *The Multi-Hyphen Life* (Kansas City: Andrews McMeel Publishing, 2020).

10. Another fun metaphor is the bento box, described by April Rinne in "Why Your Career Will Be a Japanese Bento Box, Not a 3-Course French Meal," Time4Coffee, accessed April 14, 2022, https://time4coffee.org/88-why-your-career-will-be-a-japanese-bento-box-not-a-3-course-french-meal-w-april-rinne. As she explains, different components live side by side to create a single, nourishing meal. Unlike the three-course meal, which is experienced sequentially, the bento box career can have multiple career components of varying sizes all at the same time.

11. April Rinne, "Inspirations," AprilRinne.com, accessed April 14, 2022, https://aprilrinne.com/inspirations.

12. Lisa A. Mainiero and Sherry E. Sullivan, "Kaleidoscope Careers: An Alternate Explanation for the 'Opt-Out' Revolution," *Academy of Management Perspectives* 19, no. 1 (February 2005): 106–23, https://doi.org/10.5465/ame.2005.15841962.

13. Laura Berman Fortgang, *Find Your Dream Job without Ever Looking at Your Resume*, TEDx Boca Raton, 2015, www.youtube.com/watch?v=wfNX1cHk-fE.

14. Rob Bagchi, "50 Stunning Olympic Moments No. 35: Wilma Rudolph's Triple Gold in 1960," *The Guardian*, June 1, 2012, sec. Sport, www.theguardian.com/sport/blog/2012/jun/01/50-stunning-olympic-moments-wilma-rudolph.

15. Keri Engel, "Wilma Rudolph, Olympic Gold Medalist & Civil Rights Pioneer," *Amazing Women in History* (blog), August 14, 2012, https://amazingwomeninhistory.com/wilma-rudolph-olympic-gold-medalist-civil-right-pioneer.

16. Anita Verschoth, "Slight Change of Pace for Wilma," *Sports Illustrated*, September 7, 1964.

17. "Wilma Rudolph: Olympic Gold to DePauw Gold," accessed July 12, 2022, www.depauw.edu/stories/details/wilma-rudolph-olympic-gold-to-depauw-gold.

18. Kayla Gray, interview with the author.

19. Gray.

20. Gupta, interview with the author.

21. Inna Kuznetsova, interview with the author.

22. Vyjayanthi Vadrevu, interview with the author.

23. Daniel Pinnolis, interview with the author, December 21, 2021.

24. Manya Chylinski, interview with the author.

25. Kador, interview with the author.

26. Sally Collings, interview with the author.
27. Gupta, interview with the author.
28. Pinnolis, interview with the author.
29. Paul Millerd, Interview with the author, June 22, 2022.
30. "Freelance Forward 2020."
31. Around 51 percent of freelancers had participated in skills training during the pandemic, versus 28 percent of non-freelancers, "Freelance Forward 2020."
32. Max Fucci, interview with the author, January 4, 2022.
33. Chylinski, interview with the author.
34. Kador, interview with the author; Chylinski, interview with the author; Collings, interview with the author; MacDonald, interview with the author; Fucci, interview with the author; Valverde, interview with the author.
35. Thanks to Max Fucci and Moira MacDonald for sharing these typical questions that freelancers share.
36. Kador, interview with the author.
37. Valverde, interview with the author.
38. Gray, interview with the author.
39. Ramita Ravi, interview with the author.
40. James P. Gallant, interview with the author, December 15, 2021.
41. Jordan Hayles, interview with the author, December 28, 2021.

CHAPTER 9

1. Alice Sheridan and Louise Fletcher, "Finding Time for Art & Dealing with Overwhelm," *Art Juice: A Podcast for Artists, Creatives and Art Lovers*, accessed April 10, 2022, https://podcasts.apple.com/us/podcast/finding-time-for-art-dealing-with-overwhelm-113/id1451530001?i=1000514042258.
2. Caron Barone, interview with the author.
3. *Psychology Today* staff, "Burnout," *Psychology Today*, accessed April 10, 2022, www.psychologytoday.com/us/basics/burnout; Kandi Wiens and Annie McKee, "Why Some People Get Burned Out and Others Don't," *Harvard Business Review*, November 23, 2016, https://hbr.org/2016/11/why-some-people-get-burned-out-and-others-dont; Kandi Wiens, EdD, "Leading through Burnout" (dissertation for the degree of Doctor of Education, University of Pennsylvania, 2016), www.slideshare.net/KandiWiens/leading-through-burnout-k-wiens-dissertation.
4. *Psychology Today* Staff, "Burnout."
5. Wiens and McKee, "Why Some People Get Burned Out and Others Don't"; Christina Maslach et al., "Maslach Burnout Inventory (MBI)," Mind

Garden, accessed April 10, 2022, www.mindgarden.com/117-maslach-burn-out-inventory-mbi.

6. Bstan-'dzin-rgya-mtsho and Tutu, *The Book of Joy*, 36. The quote reads: "If something can be done about the situation, what need is there for dejection? And if nothing can be done about it, what use is there for being dejected?"

7. Wiens and McKee, "Why Some People Get Burned Out and Others Don't."

8. Barone, interview with the author, edited lightly for clarity.

9. Alice Sheridan and Louise Fletcher, "Are You a Frog in Hot Water—Or When Is It Time to Delegate?" *Art Juice: A Podcast for Artists, Creatives and Art Lovers*, accessed April 10, 2022, https://podcasts.apple.com/us/podcast/are-you-a-frog-in-hot-water-or-when-is-it-time-to-delegate-20/id1451530001?i=1000440566542. This podcast series has other episodes of interest as well.

10. Danielle Langton, interview with the author, January 6, 2022.

11. Kayla Gray, interview with the author.

12. Annie Dillard, *The Writing Life* (New York: Harper & Row, 1989).

13. Pauline Rose Clance and Suzanne Ament Imes, "The Imposter Phenomenon in High Achieving Women: Dynamics and Therapeutic Intervention," *Psychotherapy: Theory, Research & Practice* 15, no. 3 (1978): 241–47, https://doi.org/10.1037/h0086006.

14. Dena M. Bravata et al., "Prevalence, Predictors, and Treatment of Impostor Syndrome: A Systematic Review," *Journal of General Internal Medicine* 35, no. 4 (April 2020): 1252–75, https://doi.org/10.1007/s11606-019-05364-1; "Tom Hanks Says Self-Doubt Is 'A High-Wire Act That We All Walk,'" *NPR*, April 26, 2016, sec. Movie Interviews, www.npr.org/2016/04/26/475573489/tom-hanks-says-self-doubt-is-a-high-wire-act-that-we-all-walk; "Michelle Obama Talks 'Imposter Syndrome,' Next Gen Empowerment & Her Own Role Models," *Vogue*, March 10, 2020, www.vogue.co.uk/arts-and-lifestyle/article/michelle-obama-on-empowering-next-generation; "Why Feeling Like a Fraud Can Be a Good Thing," *BBC News*, April 24, 2016, sec. Magazine, www.bbc.com/news/magazine-36082469; Laurieann Gibson, *Lady Gaga Presents the Monster Ball Tour at Madison Square Garden | Prime Video*, Documentary, 2011, www.amazon.com/Presents-Monster-Madison-Square-Garden/dp/B00KWH4CYG; Sandberg and Scovell, *Lean In*.

15. Ruchika Tulshyan and Jodi-Ann Burey, "Stop Telling Women They Have Imposter Syndrome," *Harvard Business Review*, February 11, 2021, https://hbr.org/2021/02/stop-telling-women-they-have-imposter-syndrome.

16. Barone, interview with the author.

17. Valerie Young, *The Secret Thoughts of Successful Women: Why Capable People Suffer from the Impostor Syndrome and How to Thrive in Spite of It*, 1st ed. (New York: Crown Business, 2011), 118–48.

18. Barone, interview with the author.

19. Carol S. Dweck, *Mindset: The New Psychology of Success* (New York: Ballantine Books, 2008).

20. Erwin Felicilda, interview with the author, June 10, 2022.

21. Sharon Stanton Russell, "Remittances from International Migration: A Review in Perspective," *World Development* 14, no. 6 (June 1, 1986): 677–96, https://doi.org/10.1016/0305-750X(86)90012-4; Adediran Daniel Ikuomola, "Unintended Consequences of Remittance: Nigerian Migrants and Intra-Household Conflicts," *SAGE Open* 5, no. 3 (July 1, 2015): 2158244015605353, https://doi.org/10.1177/2158244015605353.

22. For more on self-deprecatory humor, see Bstan-'dzin-rgya-mtsho and Tutu, *The Book of Joy*, 215–22. See also the discussion of the "beautiful-mess effect" in Anna Bruk, Sabine G. Scholl, and Herbert Bless, "Beautiful Mess Effect: Self–Other Differences in Evaluation of Showing Vulnerability—PsycNET," *Journal of Personality and Social Psychology* 115, no. 2 (2018): 192–205, https://doi.org/10.1037/pspa0000120. For the humble-brag problem, see Ovul Sezer, Francesca Gino, and Michael I Norton, "Humblebragging: A Distinct—and Ineffective—Self-Presentation Strategy," Harvard Business School Working Paper 15-080 (2017): 79.

23. Susan Scutti, "Michael Phelps: 'I Am Extremely Thankful That I Did Not Take My Life,'" *CNN*, January 20, 2018, sec. Health, www.cnn.com/2018/01/19/health/michael-phelps-depression/index.html; Meredith Day, "The Most Decorated Olympians of All Time and Their Medal Counts," *NBC New York*, July 22, 2021, www.nbcnewyork.com/news/sports/tokyo-summer-olympics/the-most-decorated-olympians-of-all-time-and-their-medal-counts/3168841.

24. Finis Jhung, interview with the author, December 22, 2021; Kador, interview with the author.

25. University of Gothenburg, "New Challenges for Ex-Olympians," ScienceDaily, accessed April 13, 2022, www.sciencedaily.com/releases/2012/09/120921083200.

26. JR Thorpe, "What Do Olympians Do After the Olympics? Their Career Paths Are as Diverse as They Are," Bustle, February 6, 2018, www.bustle.com/p/what-do-olympians-do-after-the-olympics-their-career-paths-are-as-diverse-as-they-are-7926457.

27. Jhung, interview with the author, December 22, 2021.

CHAPTER 10

1. Jennifer Liu, "Why All Your Coworkers Who Quit Are about to Come Back as 'Boomerang Employees,'" CNBC, November 3, 2021, sec. Make It—Work, www.cnbc.com/2021/11/03/great-resignation-could-fuel-the-rise-of-the-boomerang-employee.html.

2. John Choi, interview with the author, March 21, 2022.

3. Dan Pinnolis, interview with the author.

4. Ernie Valverde, interview with the author.

5. Erika Todd, email correspondence with the author," January 14, 2022.

6. Todd.

7. Max Fucci, interview with the author.

8. Matthew Huff, interview with the author.

9. The idea of bringing your whole self to work can be traced back to William A. Kahn, "Psychological Conditions of Personal Engagement and Disengagement at Work," *The Academy of Management Journal* 33, no. 4 (1990): 692–724, https://doi.org/10.2307/256287. For more on the movement to bring your whole identity, see Mike Robbins, *Bring Your Whole Self to Work: How Vulnerability Unlocks Creativity, Connection, and Performance* (Carlsbad, CA: Hay House, 2018). For examples of why doing so is harder on marginalized groups see Tomas Chamorro-Premuzic, "Bringing Your Whole Self to Work Is a Bad Idea," *Fast Company*, December 23, 2019, www.fastcompany.com/90444640/bringing-your-whole-self-to-work-is-a-bad-idea.

10. Kareem Khubchandani, interview with the author, January 26, 2022.

11. Klaus Rothermund and Christian Meiniger, "Stress-Buffering Effects of Self-Complexity: Reduced Affective Spillover or Self-Regulatory Processes?" *Self and Identity* 3, no. 3 (July 1, 2004): 263–81, https://doi.org/10.1080/13576500444000056.1985

CHAPTER 11

1. Kayla Gray, interview with the author.

2. Gray.

3. Jordan Hayles, interview with the author; Magaly Colimon-Christopher, interview with the author; Ramita Ravi, interview with the author; Danielle Langton, interview with the author.

4. Alana Massey, "How to Balance Freelance Swagger with Freelance Stigma," Fiverr Workspace, November 25, 2020, https://workspace.fiverr.com/blog/when-to-call-yourself-a-freelancer.

5. See, for example, Susan Bond, "Why I Stopped Calling Myself a 'Freelancer,'" Fast Company, December 3, 2015, www.fastcompany.com/3054141/why-i-stopped-calling-myself-a-freelancer; Melanie Padgett Powers, "Stop Calling Yourself a Freelancer," Writer's Bone, February 18, 2016, www.writersbone.com/essays-archive/2016/2/18/stop-calling-yourself-a-freelancer; Massey, "How to Balance Freelance Swagger with Freelance Stigma."

6. Timothy Butler, "Hiring an Entrepreneurial Leader," *Harvard Business Review*, March 1, 2017, https://hbr.org/2017/03/hiring-an-entrepreneurial-leader. For more than a century, people have been looking at risk and entrepreneurship. As explained in Sari Pekkala Kerr, William R. Kerr, and Tina Xu, "Personality Traits of Entrepreneurs: A Review of Recent Literature," *National Bureau of Economic Research*, working paper no. 24097 (December 2017), www.nber.org/system/files/working_papers/w24097/w24097.pdf. "Discussions of risk and entrepreneurship date back to Knight (1921), who proposes that entrepreneurs are differentiated from others by their astuteness toward perceiving and acting on opportunity despite uncertainty and risk."

7. Butler, "Hiring an Entrepreneurial Leader."

8. Ravi, interview with the author; Colimon-Christopher, interview with the author.

9. Ravi, interview with the author.

10. Jon Younger, "The Global Survey on Freelancing: Overall Results," Agile Talent Collaborative and University of Toronto, September 2021.

11. The first title, "Creative Disruptor," comes from Sarabeth Berk, interview with the author. The second title, "Director of Intellectual Creativity," comes from Hayles, interview with the author.

12. For example Ben Laker et al., "What Successful Freelancers Do Differently," *Harvard Business Review*, October 6, 2021, https://hbr.org/2021/10/what-successful-freelancers-do-differently.

13. Mark Thacker, "How Interim Executives Can Be a Surprising Benefit to Your Company," Fast Company, November 8, 2021, www.fastcompany.com/90693524/how-interim-executives-can-be-a-surprising-benefit-to-your-company; Kristin Broughton, "Demand for Part-Time CFOs Heats Up as Startups Raise More Money," *Wall Street Journal*, July 26, 2021, sec. C Suite, www.wsj.com/articles/demand-for-part-time-cfos-heats-up-as-startups-raise-more-money-11627291800; Mary Pratt, "CIOs for Hire: The Rise of the Contract CIO," CIO, accessed April 25, 2022, www.cio.com/article/304999/cios-for-hire-the-rise-of-the-contract-cio.html.

14. Adam Ozimek, "Freelance Forward Economist Report."

15. "Overemployed—Work Two Remote Jobs, Reach Financial Freedom," Overemployed, accessed April 25, 2022, https://overemployed.com.

16. Daisy Schofield, "'It's the Biggest Open Secret out There': The Double Lives of White-Collar Workers with Two Jobs," *The Guardian*, November 16, 2021, sec. Life and Style, www.theguardian.com/lifeandstyle/2021/nov/16/its-the-biggest-open-secret-out-there-the-double-lives-of-white-collar-workers-with-two-jobs.

17. For tips on avoiding micromanaging, see, for example, Amy Gallo, "7 Tips for Managing Freelancers and Independent Contractors," *Harvard Business Review*, August 17, 2015, https://hbr.org/2015/08/7-tips-for-managing-freelancers-and-independent-contractors; Chris Porteous, "How to Manage Freelancers and Independent Contractors," Entrepreneur, accessed April 25, 2022, www.entrepreneur.com/article/402493; Geoffrey Whiting, "How to Effectively Manage a Team of Freelancers," Upwork, March 25, 2021, www.upwork.com/resources/manage-team-of-freelancers.

18. Ravi Mishra, interview with the author.

19. Amy Gallo, "7 Tips for Managing Freelancers and Independent Contractors"; Whiting, "How To Effectively Manage a Team of Freelancers."

20. Chris Porteous, "How to Manage Freelancers and Independent Contractors."

21. Tommy Walker, Social Media Post, LinkedIn, January 2022, www.linkedin.com/feed/update/urn:li:activity:6887520609945964544.

22. David J. Epstein, *Range: Why Generalists Triumph in a Specialized World* (New York: Riverhead Books, 2019), 280.

23. Brian Uzzi and Jarrett Spiro, "Collaboration and Creativity: The Small World Problem," *American Journal of Sociology* 11, no. 2 (2005): 447–504.

24. Roger Guimerà et al., "Team Assembly Mechanisms Determine Collaboration Network Structure and Team Performance," *Science* (New York) 308, no. 5722 (April 29, 2005): 697–702, https://doi.org/10.1126/science.1106340.

25. Epstein, *Range*, 280.

CHAPTER 12

1. Kate Vinton, "Ringmaster of the Universe: How Billionaire Kenneth Feld Keeps Ringling Bros. Circus Alive," *Forbes*, accessed May 3, 2022, www.forbes.com/sites/katevinton/2016/11/30/how-billionaire-kenneth-feld-keeps-ringling-bros-circus-alive.

2. Jessica Lucas, "The American Circus Is in Decline, but Performers Thrive on TikTok," *Input*, January 20, 2022, www.inputmag.com/culture/circus-performers-tiktok.

3. Ramita Ravi, interview with the author.

4. Dara Silverman, interview with the author, January 21, 2022.

5. PRWeb, "Artswrk, the New Professional Network for Artists, Launches to the Public," August 2, 2021, www.prweb.com/releases/artswrk_the_new_professional_network_for_artists_launches_to_the_public/prweb18101145.htm.

6. Ravi, interview with the author.

7. Ravi.

8. "Braintrust: The Decentralized Talent Network," white paper, September 2021, www.usebraintrust.com/whitepaper.

9. For Artswrk's provision of insurance, see Artswrk, "How Do You Get Health Insurance as a Freelance Artist?" photo caption, Instagram, December 6, 2021, www.instagram.com/p/CXKLZ4wrGyA. For the Artswrk community, see Artswrk, "What Type of Artist Are You?" photo caption, Instagram, November 3, 2021, www.instagram.com/p/CV0f5gdpo_D.

10. Anne Cassidy, "Home Alone? Dealing with the Solitude of Self-Employment," *The Guardian*, May 10, 2017, sec. Guardian Small Business Network, www.theguardian.com/small-business-network/2017/may/10/home-alone-dealing-with-the-solitude-of-self-employment; Celeste Polanco, "10 Ways to Overcome Loneliness as a Freelancer," *Essence*, August 20, 2021, www.essence.com/news/money-career/10-ways-to-overcome-loneliness-as-a-freelancer.

11. Vivian Giang, "Why Isolation Is a More Serious Problem for Freelancers Than You Think," Fast Company, September 22, 2015, www.fastcompany.com/3051268/why-isolation-is-a-more-serious-freelance-than-you-think.

12. Mark Granovetter, "The Strength of Weak Ties."

13. Everett Harper, "Weak Ties Matter," *TechCrunch*, April 26, 2016, https://social.techcrunch.com/2016/04/26/weak-ties-matter/; Amanda Mull, "The Pandemic Has Erased Entire Categories of Friendship," *The Atlantic*, January 27, 2021, www.theatlantic.com/health/archive/2021/01/pandemic-goodbye-casual-friends/617839.

14. Vyjayanthi Vadrevu, interview with the author.

15. Vadrevu.

BIBLIOGRAPHY

Alboher, Marci. *One Person/Multiple Careers: A New Model for Work/Life Success*. New York: Warner Business Books, 2007.

Alton, Larry. "How Low Self-Esteem Affects Your Earning Potential." *NBC News*, November 15, 2017, sec. Better by Today. www.nbcnews.com/better/business/why-low-self-esteem-may-be-hurting-your-career-ncna814156.

American Psychological Association. "Stress in America™ 2021: Stress and Decision-Making during the Pandemic." 2021. www.apa.org/news/press/releases/stress/2021/decision-making-october-2021.pdf.

Artswrk. "How Do You Get Health Insurance as a Freelance Artist?" Photo caption. Instagram, December 6, 2021. www.instagram.com/p/CXKLZ4wrGyA.

———. "What Type of Artist Are You?" Photo caption. Instagram, November 3, 2021. www.instagram.com/p/CV0f5gdpo_D.

Associated Press. "Red Sox Fan Climbs Everest to Break Ruth's Curse." ESPN, June 20, 2001, sec. Baseball. www.espn.com/mlb/news/2001/0620/1216282.html.

Bagchi, Rob. "50 Stunning Olympic Moments No. 35: Wilma Rudolph's Triple Gold in 1960." *The Guardian*, June 1, 2012, sec. Sport. www.theguardian.com/sport/blog/2012/jun/01/50-stunning-olympic-moments-wilma-rudolph.

Baldwin, Tamala. Interview with the author, May 31, 2022.

Barone, Cara. Interview with the author, January 16, 2022.

BBC News. "What Is India's Caste System?" June 19, 2019, sec. India. www.bbc.com/news/world-asia-india-35650616.

———. "Why Feeling Like a Fraud Can Be a Good Thing." April 24, 2016, sec. Magazine. www.bbc.com/news/magazine-36082469.

Berinato, Scott. "That Discomfort You're Feeling Is Grief." *Harvard Business Review*, March 23, 2020. https://hbr.org/2020/03/that-discomfort-youre-feeling-is-grief.

Berk, Sarabeth. Interview with the author, January 10, 2022.

Bond, Susan. "Why I Stopped Calling Myself a 'Freelancer.'" Fast Company, December 3, 2015. www.fastcompany.com/3054141/why-i-stopped-calling-myself-a-freelancer.

"Braintrust: The Decentralized Talent Network." White paper, September 2021. www.usebraintrust.com/whitepaper.

Bravata, Dena M., et al. "Prevalence, Predictors, and Treatment of Impostor Syndrome: A Systematic Review." *Journal of General Internal Medicine* 35, no. 4 (April 2020): 1252–75. https://doi.org/10.1007/s11606-019-05364-1.

Brewer, Marilynn B. "The Social Self: On Being the Same and Different at the Same Time." *Personality and Social Psychology Bulletin* 17, no. 5 (October 1, 1991): 475–82.

Broughton, Kristin. "Demand for Part-Time CFOs Heats Up as Start-ups Raise More Money." *Wall Street Journal*, July 26, 2021, sec. C Suite. www.wsj.com/articles/demand-for-part-time-cfos-heats-up-as-startups-raise-more-money-11627291800.

Brown, Dawn. "How To Build Your Identity in and out of Work." *Forbes*. Accessed April 22, 2022. www.forbes.com/sites/forbesbusinesscouncil/2021/07/01/how-to-build-your-identity-in-and-out-of-work.

Brown Girl Magazine. "Slashie // Summit 2019." IFundWomen. Accessed March 27, 2022. https://ifundwomen.com/projects/slashie-summit-2019.

Browne, Ian. "Best Season Ever? Hard to Top 2004 Red Sox." MLB.com, December 26, 2021. www.mlb.com/news/classic-seasons-2004-red-sox.

Bruk, Anna, Sabine G. Scholl, and Herbert Bless. "Beautiful Mess Effect: Self–Other Differences in Evaluation of Showing Vulnerability—PsycNET." *Journal of Personality and Social Psychology* 115, no. 2 (2018): 192–205. https://doi.org/10.1037/pspa0000120.

Bstan-'dzin-rgya-mtsho, Dalai Lama XIV, and Desmond Tutu. *The Book of Joy: Lasting Happiness in a Changing World*. New York: Avery, 2016.

Bull, Marian. "The Complicated Reality of Doing What You Love." Vox, August 25, 2021. www.vox.com/the-highlight/22620178/hobby-job-leisure-labor.

Burkeman, Oliver. "The Protestant Work Ethic." *The Guardian*, September 10, 2010, sec. Life and Style. www.theguardian.com/lifeandstyle/2010/sep/11/pain-gain-work-ethic-burkeman.

Burns, David. *Feeling Good: The New Mood Therapy*. HarperCollins, 2012.

Butler, Timothy. "Hiring an Entrepreneurial Leader." *Harvard Business Review*, March 1, 2017. https://hbr.org/2017/03/hiring-an-entrepreneurial-leader.

Cameron, Julia. *The Artist's Way: 25th Anniversary Edition*. 10th edition. TarcherPerigee, 2002.

Campbell, Joseph. *The Hero with a Thousand Faces*. New York: Pantheon Books, 1949.

Cassidy, Anne. "Home Alone? Dealing with the Solitude of Self-Employment." *The Guardian*, May 10, 2017, sec. Guardian Small Business Network. www.theguardian.com/small-business-network/2017/may/10/home-alone-dealing-with-the-solitude-of-self-employment.

Catlin, Roger. "The High Wire of Going It Alone in 'One Man Circus.'" *Washington Post*, June 27, 2019, sec. Theater & Dance. www.washingtonpost.com/goingoutguide/theater-dance/the-high-wire-of-going-it-alone-in-one-man-circus/2019/06/26/15b0dd64-961c-11e9-830a-21b9b36b64ad_story.html.

Cespedes, Diony. Email correspondence with the author, January 29, 2022.

Chamorro-Premuzic, Tomas. "Bringing Your Whole Self to Work Is a Bad Idea." Fast Company, December 23, 2019. www.fastcompany.com/90444640/bringing-your-whole-self-to-work-is-a-bad-idea.

Chhabra, Divya. Interview with the author, May 25, 2022.

Chödrön, Pema. "Three Methods for Working with Chaos." Lion's Roar, January 20, 2022. www.lionsroar.com/pema-chodrons-three-methods-for-working-with-chaos.

Choi, John. Interview with the author, March 21, 2022.

Chua, Hannah Faye, Julie E. Boland, and Richard E. Nisbett. "Cultural Variation in Eye Movements during Scene Perception." *Proceedings of the National Academy of Sciences* 102, no. 35 (2005): 12629–12633.

Chylinski, Manya. Interview with the author, December 27, 2021.

Clair, Michael. "The Red Sox Once Turned to a Witch to End a Losing Streak . . . and It Worked." Cut4 by MLB.Com, October 31, 2018. www.mlb.com/cut4/red-sox-ended-losing-streak-thanks-to-witch-laurie-cabot-c299743668.

Clance, Pauline Rose, and Suzanne Ament Imes. "The Imposter Phenomenon in High Achieving Women: Dynamics and Therapeutic Intervention." *Psychotherapy: Theory, Research & Practice* 15, no. 3 (1978): 241–47. https://doi.org/10.1037/h0086006.

Cohen, Traci Bank. "Grieving the Loss of a Life You Wanted." Goop. Accessed April 22, 2022. https://goop.com/wellness/relationships/grieving-the-loss-of-a-life-you-wanted.

Colimon-Christopher, Magaly. Interview with the author, January 6, 2022.

Collings, Sally. Interview with the author, January 5, 2022.

Collins, Jim. "Good to Great." October 2001. www.jimcollins.com/article_topics/articles/good-to-great.html#articletop.

Costco. "Employees." March 2022. www.costco.com/sustainability-employees.html.

Covey, Stephen R. *The 7 Habits of Highly Effective People: Restoring the Character Ethic.* Rev. ed. New York: Free Press, 2004.

Csikszentmihalyi, Mihaly. *Flow: The Psychology of Optimal Experience.* First edition. New York: Harper & Row, 1990.

Dave, Saumya. Interview with the author, May 24, 2022.

Day, Meredith. "The Most Decorated Olympians of All Time and Their Medal Counts." *NBC New York*, July 22, 2021. www.nbcnewyork.com/news/sports/tokyo-summer-olympics/the-most-decorated-olympians-of-all-time-and-their-medal-counts/3168841.

Deakin, Michael. "Hypatia." In *Britannica*, February 25, 2022. www.britannica.com/biography/Hypatia.

Deci, Edward. "The Effects of Externally Mediated Rewards on Intrinsic Motivation." *Journal of Personality and Social Psychology* 18 (April 1, 1971): 105–15. https://doi.org/10.1037/h0030644.

Dell'Antonia, KJ. "How High School Ruined Leisure." *New York Times*, May 18, 2019, sec. Opinion. www.nytimes.com/2019/05/18/opinion/sunday/college-admissions-extracurriculars.html.

Dillard, Annie. *The Writing Life.* New York: Harper & Row, 1989.

Dimitri, David. "About." Accessed May 6, 2022. http://daviddimitri.ch/performing-artist-and-high-wire-walker.

———. Interview with the author, March 22, 2022.

Dweck, Carol S. *Mindset: The New Psychology of Success.* Ballantine Books trade pbk. ed. New York: Ballantine Books, 2008.

Engel, Keri. "Wilma Rudolph, Olympic Gold Medalist & Civil Rights Pioneer." *Amazing Women in History* (blog), August 14, 2012. https://amazingwomeninhistory.com/wilma-rudolph-olympic-gold-medalist-civil-right-pioneer.

Epictetus. *The Enchiridion.* Translated by Elizabeth Carter. The Internet Classics Archive, 135 CE. http://classics.mit.edu/Epictetus/epicench.html.

Epstein, David J. *Range: Why Generalists Triumph in a Specialized World.* New York: Riverhead Books, 2019.

Epstein, Sarah. "4 Types of Grief Nobody Told You About." *Psychology Today*, April 17, 2019. www.psychologytoday.com/us/blog/between-the-generations/201904/4-types-grief-nobody-told-you-about.

Everitt, B. S., and A Skrondal. "Regression to the Mean." In *The Cambridge Dictionary of Statistics*, 480. Cambridge, UK: Cambridge University Press, 2010.

Felicilda, Erwin. Interview with the author, June 10, 2022.

Fidelity. "Understanding the Self-Employed 401(k)." Accessed April 8, 2022. www.fidelity.com/learning-center/personal-finance/retirement/self-employed-401k.

"Flywheel." In *Britannica*. Accessed March 23, 2022. www.britannica.com/technology/flywheel.

Forte, Tiago. "The Rise of the Full-Stack Freelancer." Forte Labs, June 23, 2017. https://fortelabs.co/blog/the-rise-of-the-full-stack-freelancer.

Fortgang, Laura Berman. *Find Your Dream Job without Ever Looking at Your Résumé*. TEDx Boca Raton, 2015. www.youtube.com/watch?v=wfNX1cHk-fE.

"Freelance Forward 2020." Upwork, September 2020. www.upwork.com/documents/freelance-forward-2020.

Fucci, Max. Interview with the author, January 4, 2022.

Gallant, James P. Interview with the author, December 15, 2021.

Gallo, Amy. "7 Tips for Managing Freelancers and Independent Contractors." *Harvard Business Review*, August 17, 2015. https://hbr.org/2015/08/7-tips-for-managing-freelancers-and-independent-contractors.

Gannon, Emma. *The Multi-Hyphen Life*. Kansas City: Andrews McMeel Publishing, 2020.

Gee, Laura K., Jason Jones, and Moira Burke. "Social Networks and Labor Markets: How Strong Ties Relate to Job Finding on Facebook's Social Network." *Journal of Labor Economics*, January 26, 2017. https://doi.org/10.1086/686225.

Gelber, Steven M. In *Hobbies: Leisure and the Culture of Work in America*, 24. Columbia University Press, 1999.

Giang, Vivian. "Why Isolation Is a More Serious Problem for Freelancers Than You Think." Fast Company, September 22, 2015. www.fastcompany.com/3051268/why-isolation-is-a-more-serious-freelance-than-you-think.

Gibson, Laurieann. *Lady Gaga Presents the Monster Ball Tour at Madison Square Garden / Prime Video*. Documentary, 2011. www.amazon.com/Presents-Monster-Madison-Square-Garden/dp/B00KWH4CYG.

Gijare, Rohit. "Reminder: Be Kind to Yourself, Take a Break." Photo caption. Instagram, July 6, 2020. www.instagram.com/p/CCSVWTIl8m3.

Granovetter, Mark S. "The Strength of Weak Ties." *The American Journal of Sociology* 78, no. 6 (May 1973): 1360–80.

Gray, Kayla. Interview with the author, December 20, 2021.

Guimerà, Roger, et al. "Team Assembly Mechanisms Determine Collaboration Network Structure and Team Performance." *Science* (New York) 308, no. 5722 (April 29, 2005): 697–702. https://doi.org/10.1126/science.1106340.

Gupta, Shalene. Interview with the author, December 28, 2021.

Handy, Charles B. *The Age of Unreason*. First edition. Boston: Harvard Business School Press, 1989.

Harper, Everett. "Weak Ties Matter." TechCrunch, April 26, 2016. https://social.techcrunch.com/2016/04/26/weak-ties-matter.

Hayles, Jordan. Interview with the author, December 28, 2021.

Hicks, Coryanne. "9 Charts Showing Why You Should Invest Today." *US News*, July 23, 2018. https://money.usnews.com/investing/investing-101/articles/2018-07-23/9-charts-showing-why-you-should-invest-today.

History. "Aristotle." Accessed April 19, 2022. www.history.com/topics/ancient-history/aristotle.

History.com editors. "New York Yankees Announce Purchase of Babe Ruth." In *HISTORY*. A&E Television Networks, November 16, 2009. www.history.com/this-day-in-history/new-york-yankees-announce-purchase-of-babe-ruth.

"How Did Vincent van Gogh Become Famous after His Death?" Van Gogh Museum. Accessed July 10, 2022, www.vangoghmuseum.nl/en/art-and-stories/vincent-van-gogh-faq/how-did-van-gogh-become-famous-after-his-death.

Huff, Matthew. Interview with the author, December 27, 2021.

Hytner, Nicholas. *Center Stage*. Columbia Pictures, 2000.

Ikuomola, Adediran Daniel. "Unintended Consequences of Remittance: Nigerian Migrants and Intra-Household Conflicts." *SAGE Open* 5, no. 3 (July 1, 2015): 2158244015605353. https://doi.org/10.1177/2158244015605353.

Inflation Tool. "Value of 1971 US Dollars Today—Inflation Calculator." Accessed March 28, 2022. www.inflationtool.com/us-dollar/1971-to-present-value.

Internal Revenue Service. "One Participant 401k Plans." November 8, 2021. www.irs.gov/retirement-plans/one-participant-401k-plans.

———. "Retirement Plans for Self-Employed People." November 15, 2021. www.irs.gov/retirement-plans/retirement-plans-for-self-employed-people.

———. "Simplified Employee Pension Plan (SEP)." January 3, 2022. www.irs.gov/retirement-plans/plan-sponsor/simplified-employee-pension-plan-sep.

Jhung, Finis. *Ballet for Life: A Pictorial Memoir*. Ballet Dynamics, Inc., 2018.

———. Interview with the author, December 22, 2021.

Jhung, Jason. Interview with the author, December 24, 2021.

Kador, John. Interview with the author, December 24, 2021.

Kahn, William A. "Psychological Conditions of Personal Engagement and Disengagement at Work." *The Academy of Management Journal* 33, no. 4 (1990): 692–724. https://doi.org/10.2307/256287.

Kerr, Sari Pekkala, William R. Kerr, and Tina Xu. "Personality Traits of Entrepreneurs: A Review of Recent Literature." National Bureau of Economic Research, working paper no. 24097 (December 2017). www.nber.org/system/files/working_papers/w24097/w24097.pdf.

Khubchandani, Kareem. Interview with the author, January 26, 2022.

Kuznetsova, Inna. Interview with the author, May 11, 2022.

L'homme Cirque. "About." Accessed April 18, 2022. www.lhommecirque.com/The_One_Man_Circus/One_Man_Circus/About.html.

Laker, Ben, et al. "What Successful Freelancers Do Differently." *Harvard Business Review*, October 6, 2021. https://hbr.org/2021/10/what-successful-freelancers-do-differently.

Langton, Danielle. Interview with the author, January 6, 2022.

Lee, Victoria. Interview with the author, November 9, 2021.

Leslie, Ian. "Why Your 'Weak-Tie' Friendships May Mean More than You Think." BBC, July 2, 2020. www.bbc.com/worklife/article/20200701-why-your-weak-tie-friendships-may-mean-more-than-you-think.

Levi, Erin. Interview with the author, June 4, 2022.

Liu, Jennifer. "Why All Your Coworkers Who Quit Are about to Come Back as 'Boomerang Employees.'" CNBC, November 3, 2021, sec. Make It—Work. www.cnbc.com/2021/11/03/great-resignation-could-fuel-the-rise-of-the-boomerang-employee.html.

Long, Heather. "U.S. Now Has 22 Million Unemployed, Wiping out a Decade of Job Gains." *Washington Post*, April 26, 2020. www.washingtonpost.com/business/2020/04/16/unemployment-claims-coronavirus.

Lorraine, Chelsea. Interview with the author, May 25, 2022.

Lowe's. "Your Benefits Choices Guide." Accessed April 8, 2022. www.myloweslife.com/lowesnet/portal/enrollments/files/Linked_PDFs/Lowes_PT_EG_PDF_Final.pdf.

Lucas, Jessica. "The American Circus Is in Decline, but Performers Thrive on TikTok." Input, January 20, 2022. www.inputmag.com/culture/circus-performers-tiktok.

Lurie, David. "Graduate Job Seeking: The Rise of the 'Slasher.'" *The Guardian*, February 1, 2011, sec. Guardian Careers. www.theguardian.com/careers/careers-blog/graduate-job-seeking-the-rise-of-the-slasher.

MacDonald, Moira. Interview with the author, December 21, 2021.

Maier, Steven F., and Martin E. P. Seligman. "Learned Helplessness at Fifty: Insights from Neuroscience." *Psychological Review* 123, no. 4 (July 2016): 349–67. https://doi.org/10.1037/rev0000033.

Mainiero, Lisa A., and Sherry E. Sullivan. "Kaleidoscope Careers: An Alternate Explanation for the 'Opt-Out' Revolution." *Academy of Management*

Perspectives 19, no. 1 (February 2005): 106–23. https://doi.org/10.5465/ame.2005.15841962.

Maslach, Christina, et al. "Maslach Burnout Inventory (MBI)." Mind Garden. Accessed April 10, 2022. www.mindgarden.com/117-maslach-burnout-inventory-mbi.

Maslow, Abraham Harold. "A Theory of Human Motivation." *Psychological Review* 50, no. 4 (1943): 370.

Massey, Alana. "How to Balance Freelance Swagger with Freelance Stigma." Fiverr Workspace, November 25, 2020. https://workspace.fiverr.com/blog/when-to-call-yourself-a-freelancer.

McGrory, Brian. "Taking Teeth out of Curse?" *Boston Globe*, September 2, 2004. http://archive.boston.com/sports/baseball/redsox/articles/2004/09/02/taking_teeth_out_of_curse.

MDsave. "How Much Does an Medial Collateral Ligament (MCL) Repair Cost Near Me?" Accessed April 16, 2022. www.mdsave.com/procedures/medial-collateral-ligament-mcl-repair/d78bf8c8.

Mehra, Natasha. Interview with the author, December 17, 2021.

Merriam-Webster. "The Surprising History of 'Freelance.'" Accessed May 29, 2022. www.merriam-webster.com/words-at-play/freelance-origin-meaning.

"Michelle Obama Talks 'Imposter Syndrome', Next Gen Empowerment & Her Own Role Models." *Vogue*, March 10, 2020. www.vogue.co.uk/arts-and-lifestyle/article/michelle-obama-on-empowering-next-generation.

Millerd, Paul. Interview with the author, June 22, 2022.

Minto, Barbara. *The Pyramid Principle*. Harlow: Financial Times Prentice Hall, 2001.

Miranda, Lin-Manuel. *Tick, Tick . . . BOOM!* Based on stage musical of the same title, written by Jonathan Larson. Netflix, 2021.

Mishra, Ravi. Interview with the author, December 28, 2021.

Mull, Amanda. "The Pandemic Has Erased Entire Categories of Friendship." *The Atlantic*, January 27, 2021. www.theatlantic.com/health/archive/2021/01/pandemic-goodbye-casual-friends/617839.

Mullainathan, Sendhil, and Eldar Shafir. *Scarcity: Why Having Too Little Means so Much*. First edition. New York: Times Books, Henry Holt and Company, 2013.

Murdock, Maureen. *The Heroine's Journey*, 1st ed. Boston: Shambhala, 1990.

Norwood, Arlisha R. "Wilma Rudolph." National Women's History Museum, 2017. www.womenshistory.org/education-resources/biographies/wilma-rudolph.

Novotney, Amy. "The Psychology of Scarcity." American Psychological Association, February 2014. www.apa.org/monitor/2014/02/scarcity.

NPR. "Tom Hanks Says Self-Doubt Is 'A High-Wire Act That We All Walk,'" April 26, 2016, sec. Movie Interviews. www.npr.org/2016/04/26/475573489/tom-hanks-says-self-doubt-is-a-high-wire-act-that-we-all-walk.

O'Brien, Timothy. "When Your Job Is Your Identity, Professional Failure Hurts More." *Harvard Business Review*, June 18, 2019. https://hbr.org/2019/06/how-we-confuse-our-roles-with-our-self.

Oliver, Laura. "Is This Japanese Concept the Secret to a Long, Happy, Meaningful Life?" World Economic Forum, August 9, 2017. www.weforum.org/agenda/2017/08/is-this-japanese-concept-the-secret-to-a-long-life.

O'Shea, Arielle. "Simplified Employee Pension (SEP) IRA: How It Works." NerdWallet, March 4, 2022. www.nerdwallet.com/article/investing/what-is-a-sep-ira.

———. "What Is a Solo 401(k)? Self-Employed Retirement." NerdWallet, March 2, 2022. www.nerdwallet.com/article/investing/what-is-a-solo-401k.

Overemployed. "Overemployed—Work Two Remote Jobs, Reach Financial Freedom." Accessed April 25, 2022. https://overemployed.com.

Ozimek, Adam. "Freelance Forward Economist Report." Upwork, 2021. www.upwork.com/research/freelance-forward-2021.

Pesce, Bel. *5 Ways to Kill Your Dreams*. TEDGlobal, 2014. www.ted.com/talks/bel_pesce_5_ways_to_kill_your_dreams/transcript.

Peyton, Gabe. Interview with the author, June 1, 2022.

Pinnolis, Daniel. Interview with the author, December 21, 2021.

Polanco, Celeste. "10 Ways to Overcome Loneliness as a Freelancer." *Essence*, August 20, 2021. www.essence.com/news/money-career/10-ways-to-overcome-loneliness-as-a-freelancer.

Popova, Maria. "How Einstein Thought: Why 'Combinatory Play' Is the Secret of Genius." *The Marginalian* (blog), August 14, 2013. www.themarginalian.org/2013/08/14/how-einstein-thought-combinatorial-creativity.

Popper, Steve. "Yankees Slide to a New Low Against Indians: 22–0." *New York Times*, September 1, 2004, sec. Baseball. www.nytimes.com/2004/09/01/sports/baseball/yankees-slide-to-a-newlow-against-indians-220.html.

Porteous, Chris. "How to Manage Freelancers and Independent Contractors." *Entrepreneur*. Accessed April 25, 2022. www.entrepreneur.com/article/402493.

Post-it®. "History Timeline: Post-It® Notes." US. Accessed April 22, 2022. www.post-it.com/3M/en_US/post-it/contact-us/about-us.

Powell, Kristen. Interview with the author, May 31, 2022.

Powers, Melanie Padgett. "Stop Calling Yourself a Freelancer." Writer's Bone, February 18, 2016. www.writersbone.com/essays-archive/2016/2/18/stop-calling-yourself-a-freelancer.

Pratt, Mary. "CIOs for Hire: The Rise of the Contract CIO." CIO. Accessed April 25, 2022. www.cio.com/article/304999/cios-for-hire-the-rise-of-the-contract-cio.html.

"Protestant Ethic." In *Britannica.* Accessed April 22, 2022. www.britannica.com/topic/Protestant-ethic.

PRWeb. "Artswrk, the New Professional Network for Artists, Launches to the Public." August 2, 2021. www.prweb.com/releases/artswrk_the_new_professional_network_for_artists_launches_to_the_public/prweb18101145.htm.

Przystanski, Andy. "What Is a Career Lattice?" Lattice, September 11, 2020. https://lattice.com/library/what-is-a-career-lattice.

Psychology Today staff. "Burnout." *Psychology Today.* Accessed April 10, 2022. www.psychologytoday.com/us/basics/burnout.

Ravi, Ramita. Interview with the author, November 22, 2021.

Rinne, April. *Flux: 8 Superpowers for Thriving in Constant Change* (Berrett-Koehler Publishers, 2021).

———. "Inspirations." AprilRinne.com. Accessed April 14, 2022. https://aprilrinne.com/inspirations.

———. "Why Your Career Will Be a Japanese Bento Box, Not a 3-Course French Meal." Time4Coffee. Accessed April 14, 2022. https://time4coffee.org/88-why-your-career-will-be-a-japanese-bento-box-not-a-3-course-french-meal-w-april-rinne.

Rinzler, Lodro. *The Buddha Walks into a Bar—: A Guide to Life for a New Generation.* First edition. Boston: Shambhala, 2012.

Robbins, Mike. *Bring Your Whole Self to Work: How Vulnerability Unlocks Creativity, Connection, and Performance.* Carlsbad, CA: Hay House, 2018.

Roberts, M. B. "Rudolph Ran and World Went Wild." ESPN.com. Accessed April 14, 2022. www.espn.com/sportscentury/features/00016444.html.

Rothermund, Klaus, and Christian Meiniger. "Stress-Buffering Effects of Self-Complexity: Reduced Affective Spillover or Self-Regulatory Processes?" *Self and Identity* 3, no. 3 (July 1, 2004): 263–81. https://doi.org/10.1080/13576500444000056.

Rubin, Roger. "After Babe Ruth's Curse Was Broken, Attention Has Turned to Alex Rodriguez's Failures in the Clutch." *NY Daily News*, September 20, 2009, sec. Sports, Baseball, Yankees. www.nydailynews.com/sports/baseball/yankees/babe-ruth-curse-broken-attention-turned-alex-rodriguez-failures-clutch-article-1.406032.

Russell, Sharon Stanton. "Remittances from International Migration: A Review in Perspective." *World Development* 14, no. 6 (June 1, 1986): 677–96. https://doi.org/10.1016/0305-750X(86)90012-4.

Sandberg, Sheryl, and Nell Scovell. *Lean in: Women, Work, and the Will to Lead.* London: WH Allen, 2015.

Sargeant, Kristan. Interview with the author, December 27, 2021.

Schmidt, Victoria Lynn. *45 Master Characters: Mythic Models for Creating Original Characters*, 2012.

Schofield, Daisy. "'It's the Biggest Open Secret out There': The Double Lives of White-Collar Workers with Two Jobs." *The Guardian*, November 16, 2021, sec. Life and Style. www.theguardian.com/lifeandstyle/2021/nov/16/its-the-biggest-open-secret-out-there-the-double-lives-of-white-collar-workers-with-two-jobs.

Scott, Sir Walter. *Ivanhoe*, 1819.

Scutti, Susan. "Michael Phelps: 'I Am Extremely Thankful That I Did Not Take My Life.'" CNN, January 20, 2018, sec. Health. www.cnn.com/2018/01/19/health/michael-phelps-depression/index.html.

Sellers, Patricia. "Power Point: Get Used to the Jungle Gym." *Fortune*, August 7, 2009. https://fortune.com/2009/08/07/power-point-get-used-to-the-jungle-gym.

Sezer, Ovul, Francesca Gino, and Michael I Norton. "Humblebragging: A Distinct—and Ineffective—Self-Presentation Strategy." Harvard Business School working paper 15-080 (2017): 79.

Sheridan, Alice, and Louise Fletcher. "Are You a Frog in Hot Water—Or When Is It Time to Delegate?" *Art Juice: A Podcast for Artists, Creatives and Art Lovers.* Accessed April 10, 2022. https://podcasts.apple.com/us/podcast/are-you-a-frog-in-hot-water-or-when-is-it-time-to-delegate-20/id1451530001?i=1000440566542.

———. "Finding Time for Art & Dealing with Overwhelm." *Art Juice: A Podcast for Artists, Creatives and Art Lovers.* Accessed April 10, 2022. https://podcasts.apple.com/us/podcast/finding-time-for-art-dealing-with-overwhelm-113/id1451530001?i=1000514042258.

Silverman, Dara. Interview with the author, January 21, 2022.

Starbucks Coffee Company. "Benefits and Perks." Accessed April 8, 2022. www.starbucks.com/careers/working-at-starbucks/benefits-and-perks.

Swenson, Connor. Interview with the author, May 27, 2022.

TeamstersCare. "UPS Part-Time Benefits." May 13, 2014. www.teamsterscare.com/active-members-2/ups-part-time-benefits.

Thacker, Mark. "How Interim Executives Can Be a Surprising Benefit to Your Company." Fast Company, November 8, 2021. www.fastcompany.com/90693524/how-interim-executives-can-be-a-surprising-benefit-to-your-company.

Thorpe, J. R. "What Do Olympians Do After the Olympics? Their Career Paths Are as Diverse as They Are." Bustle, February 6, 2018. www.bustle.com/p/what-do-olympians-do-after-the-olympics-their-career-paths-are-as-diverse-as-they-are-7926457.

Todd, Erika. Email correspondence with the author, January 14, 2022.

Tovar, Josue. Interview with the author, May 29, 2022.

Tulshyan, Ruchika, and Jodi-Ann Burey. "Stop Telling Women They Have Imposter Syndrome." *Harvard Business Review*, February 11, 2021. https://hbr.org/2021/02/stop-telling-women-they-have-imposter-syndrome.

Tupper, Helen, and Sarah Ellis. *The Squiggly Career: Ditch the Ladder, Discover Opportunity, Design Your Career*. Penguin Business, 2020.

University of Gothenburg. "New Challenges for Ex-Olympians." Science-Daily. Accessed April 13, 2022. www.sciencedaily.com/releases/2012/09/120921083200.htm.

US Bureau of Labor Statistics. "Supplemental Data Measuring the Effects of the Coronavirus (COVID-19) Pandemic on the Labor Market." April 5, 2022. www.bls.gov/cps/effects-of-the-coronavirus-covid-19-pandemic.htm.

Uzzi, Brian, and Jarrett Spiro. "Collaboration and Creativity: The Small World Problem." *American Journal of Sociology* 11, no. 2 (2005): 447–504.

Vadrevu, Vyjayanthi. Interview with the author, December 23, 2021.

Valverde, Ernesto. Interview with the author, December 30, 2021.

Verschoth, Anita. "Slight Change of Pace for Wilma." *Sports Illustrated*, September 7, 1964.

Vinton, Kate. "Ringmaster of the Universe: How Billionaire Kenneth Feld Keeps Ringling Bros. Circus Alive." *Forbes*. Accessed May 3, 2022. www.forbes.com/sites/katevinton/2016/11/30/how-billionaire-kenneth-feld-keeps-ringling-bros-circus-alive.

Walker, Tommy. Social Media Post. *LinkedIn*, January 2022. www.linkedin.com/feed/update/urn:li:activity:6887520609945964544.

Whiting, Geoffrey. "How To Effectively Manage a Team of Freelancers." Upwork, March 25, 2021. www.upwork.com/resources/manage-team-of-freelancers.

Wiens, Kandi, EdD. "Leading through Burnout." Dissertation for the degree of Doctor of Education, University of Pennsylvania, 2016. www.slideshare.net/KandiWiens/leading-through-burnout-k-wiens-dissertation.

Wiens, Kandi, and Annie McKee. "Why Some People Get Burned Out and Others Don't." *Harvard Business Review*, November 23, 2016. https://hbr.org/2016/11/why-some-people-get-burned-out-and-others-dont.

Winn, Marc. "What Is Your *Ikigai*?" *The View Inside Me* (blog), May 14, 2014. https://theviewinside.me/what-is-your-ikigai/#comments.

World History Encyclopedia. "Imhotep." February 16, 2016. www.worldhistory.org/imhotep.

Young, Valerie. *The Secret Thoughts of Successful Women: Why Capable People Suffer from the Impostor Syndrome and How to Thrive in Spite of It.* First edition. New York: Crown Business, 2011.

Younger, Jon. "The Coronavirus Pandemic Is Driving Huge Growth in Remote Freelance Work." *Forbes*, March 29, 2020. www.forbes.com/sites/jonyounger/2020/03/29/this-pandemic-is-driving-huge-growth-in-remote-freelance-work.

———. "The Global Survey on Freelancing: Overall Results." Agile Talent Collaborative and University of Toronto, September 2021.

Zaagman, Elliott. "The Future of China's Work Culture." TechCrunch, October 9, 2021. https://social.techcrunch.com/2021/10/09/the-future-of-chinas-work-culture.

Zar, Rachel. "What Actually Happens to Your Body When You Stop Dancing." *Dance Magazine*, May 31, 2018. www.dancemagazine.com/rest-from-exercise.

"Zhang Heng." In *New World Encyclopedia.* Accessed April 19, 2022. www.newworldencyclopedia.org/entry/Zhang_Heng.

INDEX

abundance, mindset during, 74–75
accolades, from clients, 133
achievement, of goals, 120–21
active income, 60
The Actors Fund, health insurance through, 76
agency, as success, 102–3
The Age of Unreason (Handy), 20
ALS. *See* amyotrophic lateral sclerosis
American Psychological Association, on coronavirus pandemic, 30
amyotrophic lateral sclerosis (ALS), ix, 75–76
anxiety: management of, 113; after success, 120–21
Aristotle, 9
art careers, privilege in, 151
artistic fulfillment, commercial success relation to, 45
The Artist's Way (Cameron), 42
Art Juice (podcast), 111, 114
Artswrk, 151
automation: of discovery elements, 62; software for, 50; subcontracts for, 142; time relation to, 58–59; of to-do list, 115–16
autonomy: of fractionalized work, 144; freelancing for, 7–8, 12, 137; full-time employment lack of, 133–34; risk relation to, 127
awareness: of mortality, 31, 161n12; reflection for, 29–30

backup plan, financial, 14–15
balance, between full-time job and freelance, 128, 131, 137
Baldwin, Tamala, 16–17
Band Baaja Baaraat (movie), 53, 54, 63; goals in, 59
Barnum & Bailey circus, 149
Barone, Cara: on burnout, 112; on imposter syndrome, 116–17, 118; on self-care, 114; on windfall, 73
barriers, to freelance careers, 155; isolation as, 153; physical, 150–51; psychological, 152–53
Baryshnikov, Mikhail, 32
BDC. *See* Broadway Dance Center
Begala, Paul, 55
behavior, mindset shifted by, 158
bento box, career as, 169n10
Berk, Sarabeth, on identity, 40–41, 91–92
BetterHelp, 153
Big Apple Circus, 3
Black Swan (movie), 45

Bollywood, 45; *Band Baaja Baaraat* of, 53, 54, 59, 63; dance team, ix, x
Boston Red Sox, Curse of the Bambino on, 65, 66–67, 165n2
boundaries: breaks relation to, 52; burnout avoided by, 113, 122; enforcement of, 10, 21; as essential, 105; financial, 73–74; with passions, 48–49; for self-care, 79
Braintrust, 152
brand: of freelancer, 138; mood board representing, 128–29
breaks: to avoid burnout, 49–50; boundaries relation to, 52; pitch improved during, 70; scarcity relation to, 67–68
Brewer, Marilynn, on optimal distinctiveness, 90–91
Broadway Dance Center (BDC), 31
Brown, Dawn, on identity, 90
Brown Girl Magazine, Slashie Summit of, 39–40
Budapest, Hungary, State Academy for Circus Arts in, 3
Buddhism, 25; mortality in, 31
Buffett, Jimmy, 67
Bull, Marian, 50
bureaucracy, in traditional employment, 3, 4
burned bridges, communication to avoid, 132
burnout: boundaries to avoid, 113, 122; breaks to avoid, 49–50; identity relation to, 91, 112; self-care to avoid, 113–14; during windfall, 72
Burns, David D., on identity, 88, 89
business coach, for growth, 108
business plan: clients in, 129–30; goals for, 55–59; income streams in, 60, 63; as iterative process, 62. *See also* five-year plan

Cabot, Laurie, 66
Cameron, Julia, 42
Campbell, Joseph, xiii
capitalism: challenges from, 10; identity relation to, 88; pressures from, 47–48; Protestant ethic relation to, 84
career path: awareness in, 30; chance shaping, 31–32; crossroads in, 125–26; flexibility in, 109; freelancing to craft, 26–27, 157–58; goals in, 55–57; as hero's journey, xiii–xiv, 16, 111, 121; as jungle gym, 97; as kaleidoscope, 99; as ladder, 96–97; lulls in, 71; milestones in, 72, 79, 103; portfolio as, 19–20, 98–99, 100; role models relation to, 107; success definition in, 101–4
Carville, James, 55
caste system, in India, 84–85
celebration, of career milestones, 72, 79
Center Stage (movie), 45
Cespedes, Diony, on retirement investment, 77
chance, career shaped by, 31–32
change: of career, 26–27, 28; drivers for, *126*, 127–28, 130, 135; to five-year plan, 29
Chhabra, Divya, 8; on resilience, 23
China: notion of 996 in, 85; polymaths from, 9

Choi, John, 69, 127–28
Chylinski, Manya, 102; on learning, 105
circus: L'homme Cirque, 3–4; rise and fall of, 149–50
Cirque du Soleil, 3
civil rights activist, Rudolph as, 100
clients: communication with, 49; evaluation of, 129–30; growth of, 102; networks of, 21–22; testimonials of, 130, 133, 136; transparency with, 132
Cohen, Traci Bank, on grief, 86
Colimon-Christopher, Magaly, 45–46, 51
collaboration, innovation through, 147
Collings, Sally, 107; on financial saving, 73; on impact, 103
commercial success, artistic fulfillment relation to, 45
communication: to avoid burned bridges, 132; with client, 49; to understand goals, 146
communities: during career lull, 71; coworking spaces as, 153–54; as discovery channels, 62; as success, 102; as support systems, 105–6, 109; during windfall, 74
company-worker relationship, 145; ethical gray area in, 144
competition: in industry, 55; monetization of joy relation to, 45
conflicts of interest, between freelancing and full-time job, 131–32
consulting platforms: as discovery channels, 62; employment for, 142
consulting projects: as active income, 60; part-time, xi
conversations, about job titles, 92–93, 94, 140
coronavirus pandemic: burnout during, 49; diversification during, 55; dreams relation to, 30–31; effect on L'homme Cirque, 3–4; isolation relation to, 127; overemployment during, 145; skills training during, 170n31
costs, scarcity relation to, 68–69
coworking space, as community, 153–54
creative fulfillment, freelancing for, 5–6, 11
crossroads, in freelance career, 125–26
curiosity, in freelance mindset, 104–5
Curse of the Bambino, 65, 66–67, 165n2

daily routine, to-do list in, 111
dance team, Bollywood, ix, x
Dave, Saumya, 15–16
day job: dissatisfaction in, xiii; side hustle on top of, xii
deadlines, for goals, 57
Deci, Edward, 44
decisions, policies as, 130
delegation, 116
Dillard, Annie, 116
Dimitri, David, 149; L'homme Cirque of, 3–4
discovery elements, automation of, 62
diversification: as safety net, 55; specialization compared to, 18–19
dreams, 86; coronavirus pandemic relation to, 30–31; as wealth, 18
duality, of identity, 90–91
Dweck, Carol, 118

economic environment, effect on industry, 54
effort, in traditional employment, 17
Egypt, polymaths in, 9
Ellner, Richard, 31
emotional health, as freelancing risk, 15–16
employers: dependence on, 11, 16–17; side projects supported by, 6
employment, traditional: benefits of, 151; bureaucracy in, 3, 4; collegial nature of, 137; effort in, 17; freelance compared to, xii, xiii–xiv, 7–8, 10, 12; as ladder, 96–97; professional identity in, 133, 134–35; risks of, 16–18, 19; stability of, 157; stagnation in, 26–27; transition between freelance and, 86–87, 133–34
enforcement, of boundaries, 10, 21
entertainment industry, gatekeepers in, 149–50
entrepreneur: compared to freelancer, 138–39; mindset of, 115, 174n6
envy, of success, 120
ethical gray area, in company-worker relationship, 144
exposure, through side projects, 28
external world, change driven by, *126*, 127–28, 130, 135

failure: as learning opportunity, 118; podcasts about, 154
fears: financial risk, 20–21; about freelancing, 13–14; mortality relation to, 31; preparation relation to, 34; resilience to, 23
Felicilda, Erwin, 119
financial boundaries, 73–74
financial risk: fear of, 20–21; freelancing relation to, 14, 24; monetization of joy relation to, 46–48
financial security, as leverage, 132
financial success, 101–2
Fiverr, 138
five-year plan: freelancing in, 26–27; refusal to change, 29
fixed costs, 68–69
Fletcher, Louise, 111, 114
flexibility: in career path, 109; as essential, 31–32; of freelance work, 5, 7–8, 18, 96, 150; as success, 102–3
Flux (Rinne), 30
focus, on goals, 33–34
Focusmate, 154
Forte, Tiago, on income comparison, 60
Fortgang, Laura Berman, on kaleidoscope career, 99
401(k), self-employed, 77
freelance. *See specific topics*
Freelance Mindset, *11*
Freelancers' Union, health insurance through, 76
Fucci, Max, 104–5, 125; on leverage, 132
full-time job: freelance balance with, 128, 131, 137; freelance compared to, 141–44; lack of autonomy in, 133–34

Gallant, Jim, 108, 134
Garrido, Nate, 97
gatekeepers, in entertainment industry, 149–50
Gavin, Lee, 67
Gelber, Steven, 47

Gijare, Rohit, 163n21
Giorgio, Paul, 66–67
goals: achievement of, 120–21; communication to understand, 146; deadlines for, 57; effort for, 17; evolution of, 59; focus on, 33–34; income streams for, 60–61; in kaleidoscope career, 99; types of, 55–56, 58
Granovetter, Mark, 154
Gray, Kayla, 101, 106, 137; on automation, 62; on "zone of genius," 58
"The Greatest Show on Earth" circus, 149
Greece, polymaths from, 9
grief, in lost identity, 86–87
growth: business coach for, 108; of career, 95–96, 114–15; of clients, 102; of income, 59; of skills, 104–5; as success, 103; time investment for, 61–62
guilt, freelancer, 47
Gupta, Shalene, 45; on growth, 103; on income, 54, 102

Handy, Charles, 20
Harkness Ballet, 25
Harvard: Law School, ix–x; reunion at, 83–84
Harvard Business Review, 138
Hayles, Jordan, 108
health insurance, 15, 21, 33; as barrier to freelance career, 150–51; freelancing platforms for, 152; as self-care, 75–76
Heng, Zhang, 9
hero's journey, freelance career as, xiii–xiv, 16, 111, 121
Hero with a Thousand Faces (Campbell), xiii
hierarchy of needs, 44
hobbies: monetization of joy relation to, 50–51; as side hustle, 43
L'homme Cirque (The One-Man Circus), 3–4
Huff, Matthew, 28, 61; on autonomy, 133–34; on financial boundaries, 73–74; on freelancer guilt, 47
Hungary, Budapest, 3
hustle culture: monetization of joy relation to, 43; in United States, 84
hybridity, professional identity, 41
Hypatia, 9

identity, professional, *40*; burnout relation to, 91, 112; conversations about, 92–93; job title relation to, 85–86, 88, 91–92; market for, 54, 148; pitch of, 90–91, 92; rebirth of, 87, 94; at school reunion, 83–84; self-worth conflated with, 89; in traditional employment, 133, 134–35; types of, 40–41
ikagai ("reason for being"), 42–43, *43*, 48
illusions, about work, xiv
Imhotep, 9
immediate circle, change driven by, *126*, 127, 130, 135
impact, as success, 103
imposter syndrome: archetypes of, 117; luck relation to, 116; support systems to overcome, 118–19, 122
income: for business plan, 60, 63; growth of, 59; multiple sources

of, 11; scarcity in, 66; strategic thinking about, 54; as success, 101–2; types of, *60*, 60–61
India: caste system in, 84–85; Mumbai, x
industry: economic environment effect on, 54; milestones in, 103; shifts in, 70, 97, 99; skills relation to, 54–55
inner world: change driven by, *126*, 130, 135; well-being relation to, 126–27
innovation, through collaboration, 147
interview, job, skill pitch in, 138
investment: retirement, 77; in skills, 78; in social media, 61
isolation, 15, 21–22, 105–6; as barrier to freelancing, 153; pandemic relation to, 127
Ivanhoe (Scott), 9

Jackson, Adam, Braintrust of, 152
Jhung, Finis, 25–26; career of, 31; on learning, 121; on preparation, 32–33; on timing, 34
Jhung, Jason, 15
job loss, from recession, 16–17
job title: conversations about, 92–93, 94, 140; identity relation to, 85–86, 88, 91–92
joy, monetization of, 42; competition relation to, 45; financial risk relation to, 46–48; hobby relation to, 50–51; hustle culture relation to, 43; skills relation to, 47, 52; well-being relation to, 126
Julliard, Dimitri at, 3
jungle gym, career path as, 97, 100; role models for, 107

Kador, John, 8; on flexibility, 103; on mentors, 106; on policies, 130; on self-employment, 29; on taxes, 69
kaleidoscope career, 99, 100
Khubchandani, Kareem, 134
Kuznetsova, Inna, 49; on clients, 102

ladder, career path as, 96–97, 100; role models for, 107
Lake, Rose, 6
Langton, Danielle, 115
Larson, Jonathan, 13
"learned helplessness," 66
learning, 105; after achieving goals, 121; failure as, 118; new skills, 22, 70–71
leisure, tension between work and, 47–48
leverage, financial security as, 132
Levi, Erin, 27
Lorraine, Chelsea, 6–7; on goals, 57
losing streak, of Red Sox, 65, 66–67, 165n2
luck, imposter syndrome relation to, 116
Luna-Ostaseski, Gabe, Braintrust of, 152

MacDonald, Moira, 28, 29
Maier, Steven, 66
management, of freelancers, 145–46, 148
manager: freelancer understanding of, 138, 140–41, 148; using freelancer superpowers, 146–47
Marceau, Marcel, 3
marginalized groups, professional identities in, 134

market: changes to, 70; freelancer perspective of, 147; for professional identity, 54, 148; value in, 61
Markowitz, Harry, 19
Maslow, Abraham, hierarchy of needs by, 44
mastermind groups, to learn skills, 22
Mattel, 149
McKee, Annie, 112
Medicaid, 76
meditation, on mortality, 31, 161n12
Mehra, Natasha, 98
memento mori (awareness of mortality), 31, 161n12
mental resources, scarcity mindset effect on, 66
mentors: for freelancers, 106–7; after success, 121
Metropolitan Opera, 3
milestones, career, 72, 79, 103
Millerd, Paul: on freelancing, 32–33; on success, 104
mindset: during abundance, 74; behavior shifting, 158; during career lulls, 71; curiosity in, 104–5; of entrepreneur, 115, 174n6; as freelancer superpower, 78; during scarcity, 65–66, 74–75, 79, 119; shifted by behavior, 158; during transition, 135
Minto, Barbara, 91
Mishra, Ravi, 146
modern portfolio theory, 19
Monte Carlo, Place du Casino in, 25
mood board exercise, brand represented by, 128–29
mortality, awareness of, 31, 161n12
motivation, extrinsic or intrinsic, 44
movie production: employment for, 141; streaming platforms compared to, 143
multihyphenates, 9
multiplicity, professional identity, 41
Mumbai, India, acting school in, x
Murdock, Maureen, xiii

Nashville, Tennessee, polio treatment in, 95
National Association for the Self-Employed, health insurance through, 76
networks: client, 21–22; side projects building, 6; support, 23, 24, 33, 105–6, 109, 118–19, 122, 151; volunteer work to build, 78
New York City: Slashie Summit in, 39–40; Yankees of, 65, 67
996, notion of, in China, 85

Olympians: Phelps as, 120–21; Rudolph as, 95–96, 100, 107, 109, 168n1
optimal distinctiveness, 90–91
outsourced work, freelancer relation to, 145
overemployment, 145

part-time work: consulting projects as, xi; while freelancing, 10, 14–15, 20
passion projects: boundaries with, 48–49; cultivation of, 11
passive income, 60
Peyton, Gabe, 58
Phelps, Michael, 120–21
physical health: as barrier to freelancing, 150–51; as freelancing risk, 15, 21

Pinnolis, Dan, 102; on mood board exercise, 128–29; on well-being, 103–4
pitch: of freelance services, 140–41; of identity, 90–91, 92; improved during breaks, 70
Place du Casino, Monte Carlo, 25
platforms, freelance, 151; Fiverr as, 138; for health insurance, 152
play, self-care as, 114
podcasts: *Art Juice* (podcast), 111, 114; about failure, 154
policies: company freelance, 131; as decisions, 130; for freelancers, 155
polio, 95
polymaths, 9
portfolio, work: as career, 19–20, 98–99, 100; client testimonials for, 130, 133; discovery elements in, 62; goals for, 58; revenue compared to time in, 60
portfolio careers, 19–20, 98–99, 100; role models for, 107
Powell, Kristen, on goals, 57–58
preparation: fear relation to, 34; for freelance work, 32–33, 35
press, as discovery channels, 62
price increases, 62
privilege, in art careers, 151
professional life, reimagination of, 108
Protestant ethic, capitalism relation to, 84
The Protestant Ethic and the Spirit of Capitalism (Weber), 84
psychological health, as barrier to freelancing, 152–53

Ramirez, Manny, 67
Ravi, Ramita, 139; Artswrk of, 151; on identity, 84; on role models, 107
recession, job loss from, 16–17
The Red Shoes (movie), 25
reflection, 35; for awareness, 29–30; on monetized joy, 51
regression to the mean, in statistics, 67
relationships: between manager and freelancer, 145–46; as success, 102; success effect on, 119–20; "weak ties" as, 154
Rent (musical), 13
resilience, 23; of freelancer, 121
retirement, financial savings for, 76–77
revenue, time compared to, 60
Ringling Brothers circus, 149
Rinne, April, 30, 169n10; on portfolio careers, 98–99
risks: autonomy relation to, 127; entrepreneur relation to, 174n6; financial, 14, 20–21, 24, 46–48; of freelancing, 14–16, 24, 26; self-image relation to, 88; specialization as, 19; of traditional employment, 16–18, 19
role models, career path relation to, 107
role-playing exercise, for school reunion, 89
Romy and Michele's High School Reunion (movie), 83, 89, 93
routine, resilience through, 23
Rudolph, Wilma Glodean, 95–96, 107, 168n1; career of, 100; community of, 109
Ruth, Babe, 65, 67, 165n2

safety net: Artswrk as, 151; diversification as, 55; financial, 23, 33; freelancing as, 17; social, 15, 75
salary, capped, 17

Sargeant, Kristan, 117; on awareness, 29–30; on career change, 26–27, 28; on joy, 42; on satisfaction, 30–31
savings, financial: resilience through, 23; for retirement, 76–77; during windfall, 72–73
scarcity: breaks relation to, 67–68; costs relation to, 68–69; mindset during, 65–66, 74–75, 79, 119; skills learned during, 70–71
Schmidt, Victoria Lynn, xiii
school reunion: identity at, 83–84, 93; role-playing exercise for, 89
self-actualization, in hierarchy of needs, 44
self-care, 78; to avoid burnout, 113–14; boundaries for, 79; health insurance as, 75–76
self-employment, 29; financial risk from, 14; 401(k) for, 77. *See also* National Association for the Self-Employed
self-image, risk relation to, 88
self-worth, identity conflated with, 89
Seligman, Martin, 66
SEP IRA. *See* Simplified Employee Pension Individual Retirement Account
Shantideva, 113
Sharma, Anushka, 53
Sheridan, Alice, 111, 114
Shut Up & Write, 154
side hustle, 51; hobbies as, 43; for student loans, 5; on top of day job, xii
side projects: exposure through, 28; network built by, 6
Silverio, Nick, Artswrk of, 151
Silverman, Dara, 151
Simplified Employee Pension Individual Retirement Account (SEP IRA), 77
singularity, professional identity, 41
skills: of freelancer, 17–18, 139, 140; growth of, 104–5; imposter syndrome relation to, 118; industry relation to, 54–55; investment in, 78; learning new, 22, 70–71; monetization of joy relation to, 47, 52; pitched in job interview, 138; portfolio relation to, 98; training during coronavirus pandemic, 170n31
"slashies," 9, 39–40, 168n9
Slashie Summit, 39–40
Smith, Alex, 26; on reasons to freelance, 4
social media: client communication on, 49; as discovery channel, 62; investment in, 61; psychological health resources on, 153
software: automation, 50; expense tracking, 69
specialization, diversification compared to, 18–19
Spectrum of Project Types, *141*
Spiro, Jarrett, 147
stability, of employment, traditional, 157
State Academy for Circus Arts, Budapest, 3
statistics, *regression to the mean* in, 67
stigma, of freelancing, 138–39
Stoicism, mortality in, 31
stopgap measure, freelancing as, 5
streaming platforms, employment for, 143
stress, management of, 112–13

student loans, side hustle for, 5
subcontracts: for automation, 142; management of, 145–46
success: agency as, 102–3; anxiety after, 120–21; artistic fulfillment relation to, 45; effect on relationships, 119–20; financial, 101–2; relationship, 102; well-being as, 103–4
Sudo, Kenji, 25
superpowers, of freelancers: job title to pitch, 140; manager using, 146–47; mindset as, 78
support systems, 33; communities as, 105–6, 109; to overcome imposter syndrome, 118–19, 122; as privilege, 151; resilience through, 23, 24
Swenson, Connor, 73

Talkspace, 153
taxes: financial saving for, 73; for freelancers, 69
tech industry, side projects supporting, 6
TED talk, of Fortgang, 99
television production: employment for, 142; streaming platforms compared to, 143
Tennessee, Nashville, 95
testimonials, of clients, 130, 133, 136
therapy, accessibility of, 153
Thorpe, J. R., 121
Three Areas Driving Change, *126*, 126–28, 135
Tick, Tick . . . Boom! (movie), 13; false dichotomy in, 20
time: automation relation to, 58–59; investment of, 61–62; revenue compared to, 60
timing, of freelance leap, 34
Todd, Erika, 131–32
to-do list: automation of, 115–16; in daily routine, 111
Tovar, Josue, freelancing as financial opportunity for, 4–5
transition: mindset during, 135; between traditional employment and freelance, 86–87, 133–34; of working life, 150
transparency: with clients, 132; in traditional employment, 135

Uber, company-worker relationship of, 144
United States: hustle culture in, 84; social safety net in, 15, 75
Upwork, skills training research by, 104
Uzzi, Brian, 147

Vadrevu, Vyjayanthi, 14; on community, 102
Valverde, Ernie, 6, 106, 131; on famine times, 71
Van Gogh, Vincent, 45
variable costs, 68–69
vision board, mood board compared to, 128
volunteer work, network built by, 22, 78
Vox (news site), Bull article in, 50

Walker, Tommy, 147
"weak ties" relationships, 154

wealth, dreams as, 18
Weber, Max, 84
well-being: inner world relation to, 126–27; as success, 103–4
WeWork, 154–55
Wiens, Kandi, 112
windfall: burnout during, 72; communities during, 74; effect on relationships, 119–20; financial saving during, 72–73
work: fractionalized, 144; illusions about, xiv; tension between leisure and, 47–48
working life, transition of, 150

Yankees, New York, Curse of the Bambino relation to, 65, 67
Young, Valerie, 117

"zone of genius," 58

ABOUT THE AUTHOR

Joy Batra is the founder of Quartz Consulting, a freelance consulting firm that has advised start-ups, venture capital firms, and Fortune 500 companies. She previously worked at Goldman Sachs, Gunderson Dettmer, JioSaavn, and—briefly—as a Bollywood actress. Joy spends her days building the future of investing at Syndicate Protocol. In her free time, she dances enthusiastically with minimal technique. Joy has lived or worked in India, Indonesia, South Korea, Thailand, the UAE, and the UK, but she calls Boston home.

CPSIA information can be obtained
at www.ICGtesting.com
Printed in the USA
BVHW041137021122
650042BV00004B/12

9 781538 167700